The PROCLIVITY *of* TIME

DARNELL WHITTINGTON

ISBN 978-1-63844-826-6 (paperback)
ISBN 978-1-63844-827-3 (digital)

Christian Faith Publishing, Inc.
832 Park Avenue
Meadville, PA 16335
www.christianfaithpublishing.com

Scripture quotations are taken from the King James Version of the Holy Bible, Oxford printed at the University Press London in 1876; Henry Frowne Oxford University Press warehouse 7, New York, 42 Bleecher Street.

Proclivity is natural or habitual inclination or tendency of *Selah*: to pause and think reflectively about it.

Cover explanation: This picture represents a contrast to the proclivity of time or the natural course of time, thereby demonstrating the power of God and showing time from God's perspective. From our perspective, time is running out; but from God's perspective, time is filling up, hence the fullness of time. Even though things seem to be falling apart, in reality, everything is just coming together for the fulfillment of God's plan to restore the earth and His creation.

Printed in the United States of America

DEDICATION

FIRST AND FOREMOST, THIS BOOK is dedicated to the creator of time.

Secondly, this book is dedicated to my son, Justice, my wife, Anita, and the rest of my family and friends.

Thirdly, this book is dedicated to Dr. Roy Higgins, Dr. Jim Woods, Sara, Adam, and Mark Woods. These are people who believed in me and gave me a chance.

Last but not least, I dedicate this book to my parents, Charles and Darlene Whittington, for without them, my time on earth wouldn't be possible.

CONTENTS

To everything there is a season, and a time to every purpose under the heaven: a time to be born, and a time to die; a time to plant, and a time to pluck up that which is planted; a time to kill, and a time to heal; a time to break down, and a time to build up; a time to weep, and a time to laugh; a time to mourn, and a time to dance; a time to cast away stones, and a time to gather stones together; a time to embrace, and a time to refrain from embracing; a time to get, and a time to lose; a time to keep, and a time to cast away; a time to rend, and a time to sew; a time to keep silence, and a time to speak; a time to love, and a time to hate; a time of war, and a time of peace.

—Ecclesiastes 3: 1–8

ACKNOWLEDGMENTS

I WOULD LIKE TO SAY "Thank you to the Holy Spirit," for I know not what I ought to know; my understanding is limited to where I am. My thoughts are only small clusters of my finite experiences. My ideas are borrowed and unproven to withstand the variances of life. I know nothing but what has stood the test of time, and even in this, I am still left with questions. Yet through all of this, the Holy Spirit gives me what I need to know when I need to know it.

INTRODUCTION

THE PROPER RESPECT FOR TIME is the beginning of success in all things. The value of time, to most people, is not realized until it is too late. Most of our lives are wasted due to being unconscious of how short life truly is. There is an irony in the deaths we experience in life, in that death acts as a speed bump that reminds us of the things that are truly important. This reflection causes us to consider time, specifically the time we have left. There is only so much that is given, and when it is used up, there are no refills or redoes. We must move on to the next thing, regardless if we feel finished or not. Our experience with time always has us at the start of something, in the middle of something, or at the end of something. We should always gauge where we are based on the time we have or the time we think we have left. Time moves us to the end of whatever is started within us which makes time necessary in order to accomplish or achieve the things we were destined for.

The proclivity of time or the natural course of time flows in one direction, uninterrupted until the fullness of time. Along this timeline is where we exist, and beyond this timeline is where we shall exist once again as a spirit in eternality. We are here for a season, and the life and time we have has been forged with meaning. The reason we are here and the time we have been given are used together to help us accomplish our God-given purpose here on the earth. Within the pages of "The Proclivity of Time," we will discover where time is taking us, and for what reason, and we will identify the giver and keeper of time. We will determine the value that should be placed in time, and we will also experience time through moments penned to capture the very essence of what being alive is really about in such times as these. Time is winding down for some, and at the same time, it is winding up for others. It will be the end for some (forever separated from God, spiritual death), and it will be a new beginning for others (new heaven and new earth forever with God, spiritual life).

The scenes of life are being played out right before our eyes, and the things once foretold to happen are happening as predicted at their appointed time. Time is facilitating the will of God, and we must not allow ourselves to be lost in time because time has no meaning to the lost, but to those of us who are conscious, time is intentional. In my experience with God, it seems as though timing is calculated and intricate in everything. It is important to note that how God sees time and how we see time may differ based on perspective. From our perspective (from where and how we see), time is running out; but from God's perspective (from where and how he sees), time is filling up, hence the phrase "the fullness of time." The end of things spoken of in the beginning is coming together to bridge the end to a new beginning. In other words, even though things seem to be falling apart, in reality, everything is just coming together for the fulfillment of God's plan to restore the earth and His creation.

This is "The Proclivity of Time."

CHAPTER 1

Time always tells a story.

A Lifetime

As WE LIVE, TIME UNVEILS the chapters of our life's story. Sara and Roy met in high school, and one could say that it was love at first sight because they later married and lived with each other for over sixty years. During that time, they experienced having their first child, who would later be one of seven children. One day, they watched their children crawl; and then the next day, it seemed their children were off to college. Before long, fiancés and grandkids filled their home with love as they celebrated the birth of Jesus the savior during the Christmas holidays. Year after year, their family grew. They experienced joy at each birth and overwhelming sadness at the death of one of their children. For months, they expressed that parents aren't supposed to bury a child and that it was only right for the parents to depart first. As time kept its steady course, they grew to accept the course life had given them.

Overall, life for them had been good, but not without the many challenges in their health, finances, children, and even their marriage. They experienced together the sleepless nights, praying for a wayward child's struggle with addiction which almost cost him his life and family. They have been there for each other during the death of each other's parents. They have lost jobs and have experienced natural disasters together. They have lost everything and had to start over; they have been in an automobile wreck and have unexplainably survived. They have found themselves in several situations that only God could have gotten them through. During the course of time, they have seen change and have changed themselves, in the same direction, mainly around their waistline. Life had been full of victories and failures, but through it all, their love and commitment to God and each other had made them inseparable. Sixty or so years later, when talking, they finish each other's sentences, and they seemed to have the ability to communicate without saying a word in front of others; they knew each other's thoughts. Everything they did was always with each other from going to bed and waking up and to holding hands while grocery shopping. As the old saying goes, "They were joined at the hip"—that is, until time invited a guest that always seems to somehow take us all by surprise, a guest that always seems to take one and leave the other.

At this point in their lives, they would have been okay with this visitor called death, but he said that he was only there for one of them. To these two lovebirds, separation from each other was death within itself. Holding hands, they stared death in the face as Roy contemplated life by saying, "A lifetime is a short time now it seems." As life slowly eased away and the transition set in, before he took his last breaths, he said, "I will love you forever." Surrounded by their children and grandchildren, Sara, with Roy's hand still in her hand, turned to her children to say, "Now, he is truly at peace." She, somehow, maintained her joy in anticipation of seeing Roy once again. It was almost as if they were engaged again, and Roy went ahead to prepare a place for them. After getting all of their business in order, to everyone's surprise, Sara joined Roy just four months later. Their children all said that they could never stand to be apart, so this shouldn't have been a surprise. Four months later, at heaven's gates, surrounded by family and friends, Sara saw Roy again as they beheld the glory of the One who was at the center of their love story. I'm sure Sara and Roy reflected on how short the time could be but were thankful for all of the moments that made their life meaningful and good. As they stood together looking back through time, they laughed and said that it was indeed a good day. They had a wonderful life, but when the season changes, so must we. Seasons exist within the boundaries of time, and God sets the seasons according to his appointed time.

The time within the seasons have degrees of preparation that develop and equip us for the journey and destination ahead.

A lifetime is only a moment of change in comparison to eternity, and that moment of change was meant to be enjoyed within the boundaries the Father has set before us. Where the moment ends, eternity begins, and then forever in Him shall our, those that belong to Him, joy be.

In Time

The time that is given to us in life is but a moment, a breath of air, a vapor, and the wind that comes and suddenly goes. In time, we all were born; and in time, we all shall shed this earthly tent. Time is the thing that keeps us here on earth, and in time, it will be the very thing that escorts us away. It is a constant and continuous occurrence that moves and is only noticed after it has passed. It can only be measured by the change that is seen, such as the constant states of change found in life which makes up our days, nights, months, years, seasons, situations, and circumstances. Things are never revealed to us all at once, but in time, everything that is concealed in time that needs to be known shall be revealed.

I have observed some of the characteristics of time, and I have concluded that time can be managed, but it can never be conquered. It is as water one tries to hold in his or her hand only to eventually seep away. It is a force that can be governed but never stopped. It can be tracked but as the wind, never caught. It can be calculated but never figured. It can be wasted but never regained. It can be forgotten, yet it always remains. It never pauses or hesitates out of respect for the dead. "As another bites the dust," it moves on full steam ahead. It is the order in man's chaos moving us to the main event. The only control we have over it is how we experience it and what we do with it. Nevertheless, time isn't forever; one day, it's promised to be no more. Time is just an interruption in eternality; and through our experiences with it, we will be able to see and measure a glimpse of God's mercy, patience, and justice.

As faithful as the rising of the sun and the setting that ends the day, time on earth exists continuously whether we are here or not, and it shall continue long after we are gone if the Lord tarries. Where time begins and ends is a mystery to mankind. It is almost like one of those things, such as where does the wind come from and where does it go? Who sets time and the measurements of its length in our lives? Who gives us the number of our days? That indeed is something to think about or ponder because the answer to these questions would reveal the one in which deserves our devotion. He would be the one that deserves our time.

Throughout time, men have flirted with the notion of finding the fountain of youth so that they could live forever on earth. Time is, indeed, simply moments of change, and to find the power to suspend it would make one a deity of some sort because one would have to hold everything in place as he or she stops the earth from rotating on its axis. You see, time is constant movement; days are measured from an earthly perspective by the rising and the setting of the sun, but in fact, we are spinning on our axis and rotating around the sun in a circular motion. Here, we see an example of a cycle that depicts a beginning and an ending only to start all over again. This begs the question of "Does life ever end?" The answer is no; we simply transition from one state to another, from one ending to a new beginning. We are, in our truest form, eternal spirit-beings having an earthly experience.

We are sojourners in a distant land; we are just in this world but not of it. In a sense, with the approval from the Almighty, we have been given a passport to function legally within the borders of the earth realm. To illustrate this, astronauts need space suits to go to foreign lands in space. Without their suit, they could not survive the environment. The same goes for us because, as spirits, whose origin is from God, we are in a foreign land called earth. In order to survive the environment or have authority to function in the earth, we too must put on a suit. Even Lucifer (the devil) had to borrow a body (the serpent) in order to legally operate in the earth—a body in which he used to facilitate the fall of man. God also, when he came to the earth in the form of Jesus, had to put on an earth suit (flesh) to function legally and fulfill the purpose for which He came. Like all suits that are governed by time, someday, our temporary suits will wear out, and our spirits must separate from our body of flesh (which is the definition of death) and return home from which spirits come from. *Death is just a separation from our purpose of being here on the earth.* As long as we have breath in our lungs and a body for our spirits, there is purpose and work to be done in the earth. Now, eternal death is another story; it is the separation of our spirits from God which is the worse death someone can experience. Despite the literal descriptions we have heard of, this is the worst part of hell.

Revelation on Life

We live. We die. We wonder. We fear why. We gain. We lose. We're forced. We choose. We smile. We frown. We're up. We're down. We laugh. We cry. We live. Loved ones die. We succeed. We achieve. We doubt. We believe. We hurt. We shatter. We live. We matter. We talk. We fight. We hate. We might. We love. We embrace. We worry. We face. We struggle. We obtain. We forget. We blame. We live. We lie to ourselves, thinking we have more time. Then we die.

Preparation for Life After This Life Is What Really Matters.

Unfortunately, this notion of suspending time and prolonging our lives in this realm, by some, has not been well thought out. Living forever creates a new set of problems beyond the fantasy of immortality on earth in this existing form. As depicted in the 2015 film, "The Age of Adaline," what would be the point of living forever in this life if no one else could? A man once said that, "If you live in a place long enough, you will experience the sorrow of that place." To live forever would mean that you would be conscious to and experience the heart break of losing everyone you will ever love. To live unchanged in a realm of constant change, to me, does not seem to be a fountain worth drinking from. After all, dying or changing from one state to another is a part of the living experience, and what does not change is already dead in this realm. How could one appreciate life in the absence of death? The polarity of life and death within themselves yield the definition that they are opposites; and what bridge the two on earth is time.

Time conceals the answers to our questions from the beginning to the end. Time reminds us all that someday we all will have to say goodbye to this realm and enter the realm from which we came. Time holds most of what there is to know; the rest we shall know once we reach the borders beyond the end. Oh, the wonder that if viewed closely one could find in this life! There are many mysteries yet to unfold and many stories yet to behold.

Beyond the borders of time in a place called eternity. It is a place where events are beyond measure. Life and death are forever separated. At the same time, within the realm of time, things are constantly changing which, in my opinion and possibly the angels that witnessed creation, is the thing that make this life and living interesting. The fact of never knowing what the change engrained in time will bring defines the very essence of what living within the borders of time is—a journey with a beginning and, ultimately, an end meant to fulfill a divine purpose.

It is clearly obvious that eternality is perfect, yet in the messiness and unpredictability of time, there seems to be a hint of genus and a dash of perfection hidden within its imperfections. Who is the mastermind behind this complex concept of time? What exactly is it? In time, we all will soon know.

Selah 1:1–44

1. Time is the measure of events against one another, and we truly never know the value of that time until it becomes a memory.
2. We never know how precious time is until there is none left to spend.

3. Everything is impossible until someone does it. What we become is determined by how we spend our time. If we do nothing with our time, in time, we will never do anything. If we invest our time into something worthwhile, time will be a witness to the fruits of our labor and reward us.

4. As we reflect on last year, we generally examine where we are compared to where we were. The word *new* is a word for *reset*. When a computer program is not working right sometimes, we have to reset or reboot it. A new day gives us a chance to change things and an opportunity to make what's wrong right or to put what off course back on course. A new year can give us an opportunity to change the direction of our lives. It is a benchmark in which we make assessments of how well or not so well we have done. A new year give us a chance to reset our priorities in order to improve the outcome of our future. Always remember that the battle is lost or won daily, so we must maintain the excitement that we all have when embarking on a new journey. We must treat each day as if it is the finish line to us accomplishing our goals. The only way to accomplish our resolutions is to faithfully take the steps daily required to get us there.

5. Death is as being born into a new realm or world. Picture a baby in the snuggling comforts of his mother's womb. The baby was not created to stay there. Eventually, the environment gets uncomfortable as he grows. Room is limited; the fluid that sustains his life in that environment disappears, and the pressure to get out presses upon him. Once out, his source to life in that environment is cut off as a life and world unknown to him is revealed. Such as death to the environment in which we live in upon the earth, the pressure to get out presses upon us as our breath becomes faint. Finally, as we are born to a new realm or world, we are cut off from the body that was the sustainer of our life, and a life and world unknown to us is revealed. Death is as being born again into a new place.

6. Memories are moments captured in time. As time passes, those moments can begin to fade away, if not revisited from time to time.
7. We are as dead men walking, bones awaiting to be collected, a memory waiting to be forgotten. Life is meaningless without the purpose of God attached to it.
8. We have to learn to be present in the moment because those are precious moments.
9. What do we do when we have prayed for something time and time again, but we see nothing! Trust God! Sometimes, the answers don't reveal themselves when and how we want them to.
10. We can't halt time, but like water, we can determine where it goes.
11. Each day is a gift; the older I get, the more I understand the importance of opening all my gifts with joy now before the party is over.
12. Out of the blue, my wife told me that I was a good guy; I was like wow! I am? Thanks, baby! She then said, "Yea, a good guy with a lot of issues," to which I replied, "Yea, and you are one of them." Acting like an old couple, we both laughed!
13. What is the number one thing that causes a struggle in marriages? False expectations. We all go into marriage with a dream of what marriage will be like. The bottom line is that marriage is work, and what we put into it is what we will get out of it. We can't go into it with these preconceived false expectations and conditions. The struggle comes in when our spouse can't live up to these often time unrealistic expectations and conditions. We set ourselves up for failure when we do this because what happens when our spouse does not meet our expectations and conditions? Resentment begins to fester, causing a barrier within the marriage. The only thing we should expect from our spouses is for him or her to be who they are, but we can inspire him or her by how we respond to them. Always

remember that true love isn't based on conditions, but it is based on a commitment to die to ourselves for the sake of our commitment. No one ever said love would be easy. It actually makes us vulnerable and susceptible to being hurt. In its true form, it is a sacrifice expecting nothing in return. It is not a feeling which is just a by-product, but it is a choice. Also, we can't give someone something we don't have. In order to be capable of properly loving someone else, we must first love ourselves. *We must first know our value so we can see that same value in others. This is accomplished by understanding God's love for us and the value he placed on us by sacrificing himself (his son) because of His love for us.* So what? We should decide to love and serve our spouse with wisdom, knowledge, and understanding today as if we are serving the Lord. This takes the sting out of the sacrifice. Learn what love is to each other. Love never fails, and it can resurrect a dead marriage. It can save us the devastation of having our hearts ripped out still while beating and having to forfeit everything we've built only to start over. Time is short, so before we decide to go looking for someone better, we must look in the mirror and become someone better ourselves. It begins with us; we must avoid the temptation of false expectations and conditional love! Marriage is about sacrifice, and there is just something in us that must die in order for it to work. Sometimes, we may feel like the chicken giving up our eggs, and there are sometimes we may feel like the pig giving up our bacon. Some days, we will be the bug; and other days, we will be the windshield. Either way, marriage can be messy; and it requires unconditional love, selflessness, and forgiveness to reach longevity. If we serve (maybe not equal at times but equable based on capacity) each other as serving the Lord, the roots of our marriage will grow deep and nourish our whole house. The fruit our trees will bear will be a blessing for all to partake of and admire.

14. When we were young, we always wanted to go do something even though we had no money. Now that we are older and have a little money, we pay to go do nothing. Oh, the irony.

15. When God provides for us, He has more than us in mind. Love is a gift that we all should give.

16. The cemetery is always a quiet place. There is not much traffic there, and its residents are always at home. The funny thing is that no one wants to stay there. Thank God we don't have to!

17. Planning is a guard against wasted time.

18. Instead of asking ourselves what's wrong with me, focus on and ask ourselves, What's right with me?

19. Those that have and won't give are truly the ones less fortunate.

20. The Word of God is not limited by time.

21. There is not much time to waste; seventy to eighty years is not much time to travel down the same roads three and four times. We should read the signs, heed the warnings, go the speed limit (pace yourself), keep your eyes on the road, rest when needed, and revisit the mapping of your destination. We should stop and make sure we are on the right road as often as we can. We shouldn't take unnecessary detours because some people never find their way back to the main road.

22. The only perfect moment in time can only be experienced once it stops or starts.

23. All of heaven is behind God's words. We should be also.

24. Courage is not without the company of fear, but it is without the paralysis that causes inaction.

25. Life consists of moments that if we enjoy them, we will someday look back and say life was good.

26. A mirror is one thing that will never lie to us; time catches up to us all for all to see.

27. People don't so much resist change. They resist being changed in regards to how it with affect them. It is the fear

of the unknown that causes people to push back on the progressive effects of time.

28. Man can only survive forty days without food, twelve days without sleep, six days without water, and five minutes without oxygen. Man cannot survive one moment without God.

29. Everything done by God is based on His timing and not our expectations.

30. Life is a passage of entering and going out. Everything arrives on time, and everything expires when it is out of time. A long life is still a short time.

31. The end of something is only the beginning of something else.

32. We can climb to the top, but at some point, we will have to climb down. The journey down will depend on the path we took on the way up. A man of integrity and character even his enemies will respect him in his descend.

33. We should never allow ourselves to be in the position where everything changes but us. It is the beginning stages of giving up on life. Our growth and longevity are determined by how well we adapt to change.

34. Life can be risky but without the risk. What is life? The pursuit of something is what makes us feel alive. Better to have lived and have risked it all than to have lived without truly living.

35. Hidden are the treasures that wait for discovery inside a man. A man's gift is hidden from him until an appointed time for him to develop and use it. When a man's gift, time, and purpose collide, there is a huge impact in the earth that last for generations. A man's gift used to its fullness will outlive that man.

36. For most people, with age comes sensibility; but a fool will, more than likely, always be a fool.

37. How does time heal old wounds? Time separates us from our memories. If what hurts us, in our minds, no longer

exist, it can no longer hurt us. This is why time can heal old wounds.

38. Since the beginning of time, a man has always been a man, and a woman has always been a woman; I don't know what ever happened to common sense, but I bet you that I can't convince you that an apple is an orange or a dog is a cat. Each has their own purpose and identity, and such as man.

39. At some point in our lives, we will be able to see and understand how short of a time we have here on earth. As we stare our own mortality in the face, we can see how short of a time we have to do what we are meant to do. I'm told that there is a point where we no longer fear dying, but it is living that becomes frightful.

40. We came here with nothing and we will leave here with nothing; the value of our time here will be found in what we leave behind once we have gone. Legacy!

41. We can be right in our stance, but if love is not holding us up in our stance, everything we stand for will fall on deaf ears.

42. Our past is like a pencil without an eraser. We can't erase it, but thank God, we can scratch through it.

43. Blood requires blood, and one way or the other, the price shall be paid. If life matters, then all lives should matter and should be protected. I support life with no exceptions; why? Because we are more than just flesh and blood. We are spirits sent here by God with meaning and a purpose. The vehicle in which we arrived matters not; every life matters and is precious to God. Even in the worst circumstance, there is a purpose behind why God breathed life into that vessel—even broken vessels. He put something in them to get something significant out of them. I ponder the fact why those who vehemently scream their opposition to life don't stop to consider that they themselves could have been a victim of their own ideology. How do they justify taking the breath of God from others while they have been spared theirs? Is this really about a women's right to choose what

they want to do with their bodies? Do they dare assume the position of God over another life, choosing its beginning and its brutal end? Yes, we have inalienable God-given rights, but taking that which belongs to God is not one of them. As in the story of Cain, the first murderer, and Abel, the shedding of innocent blood cries up to God. The sin of it cannot be hidden, yet it shall speak, and the voice of the Almighty shall ask continuously to those who shed innocence blood, "Where is thy brother?" No, we don't have a right to choose death for someone else simply because we chose to. We are our brothers' keeper which mean we are all called to protect the sanctity of life. Life is sacred to God, and it should be sacred to all of us who have the opportunity to live it.

44. As I contemplate the situations of some of the people around me, I can't help but think of how foolish I have been. We have to learn to take inventory or as the old people used to say, "Count your blessings." As the old saying goes, "I stopped complaining about my shoes when I saw the man with no feet." I will add to this. I stopped complaining about my job when someone close to me lost their job. I stopped complaining about my children and held them tight when someone I know buried their child unexpectedly. I stopped complaining about my spouse when my neighbor's spouse was injured and now can't do anything for herself. I stopped complaining about my pastor when I found myself in a seemingly hopeless situation and my "friends" deserted me, but he was there. I stopped complaining about that old dog up the street when he alerted me to someone trying to break into my home. I stopped complaining about what I didn't have when I saw that homeless man on the corner who had nothing but the riddled shirt on his back. I stopped complaining about my life when I heard a classmate of mine, who has a wife and young children who needs him, got a diagnosis that could possibly end his life. Of course, not all of this has happened

to me, but my point is that there are so many things we could be thankful for regardless of our situation. There is always someone out there worse off than us. The only way out of the wilderness is through praise. A thankful heart transforms seemingly impossible situations into possible situations. A thankful heart puts the wind of joy back into the sails of life. This joy is the grace and strength we all need to walk in victory. Lord, forgive me for my complaining! "For I know that all things work together for good to them that love you and are called according to your purpose" (Romans 8:28).

CHAPTER 2

What Exactly Is Time?

THE PROCLIVITY OF TIME, THE nature of time, or the arrow of time flows from the beginning to the ending in one direction according to British astrophysicist Arthur Eddington in 1927, but according to Ecclesiastes 1:9, "What has been is what will be, and what has been done will be done again; there is nothing new under the sun." Time, although it flows in one direction, is somewhat circular in nature in that everything tends to end up where it first started. This loop pattern seen in time is surrounded by everything else eternal. Time repeats itself, not separate to but as a part of eternity which is the incomprehensible concept we call forever. Yet and still, the time that governs humanity has an expiration date, an appointed time that only the creator knows. The purpose that we have been given on earth must be accomplished in a certain timeframe, and at the end of this age, the overall purpose of humanity shall be revealed for all to know; this is called the fullness of time.

The origins of time and its purpose to many is somewhat perplexing, and one definition of it doesn't seem to quite cover the complexity of the concept of time. It is said to be the measure in which we order events from the past, present, and the future, as well as the space between events. It is an abstract in which we only see the evidence of its existence through the changes that occurs between spaces of consciousness. Time is how we describe observed change; but if time is made up of the past, present, and the future, then it could be implied that without time, everything that happened, is happening, and will happen would happen all at once. I believe this is what eternity is like; there is no separation of the past, present, and the future, and everything that was known, is known, and shall be known has always been known. Time is what separates us from eternality. I think this is the beginning of the understanding of the state of eternity, a circle of events whose ending and beginning exist in the same moment. The story of life began with the ending and then crossed over to the beginning with hints of how the story shall end within the context of earth. In reality, the story of life on earth is a never-ending story, much like a circle that chases itself until something greater intervenes. The concepts of time and eternity is complex but intriguing to say the least.

As human beings, much like everything else, we were created on purpose for a purpose. Understanding time helps us to understand the limitation of our purpose here on earth. It is the key that helps position us to fulfill or move us toward that purpose. As human beings, we have been given time, which is attached to an assigned divine purpose. Our time is just a piece of a bigger puzzle and a part of everything in which explains our existence.

According to Kari Enqvist, a professor of cosmology, the concept of time began with the big bang. Scientists, including Stephen Hawking the famous theoretical physicist, have concluded that there was no space or time before the big bang. According to Stephen Hawking, "The conclusion of this lecture is that the universe has not existed forever, rather the universe, and time itself, had a beginning in the Big Bang." On a side note here, why do people pray to the universe as if it is a god? Can a god such as this be created? Apparently, so! This conclusion by the scientist suggests that space and time had a beginning, and the beginning started about 13.7 billion years ago with an explosion of compressed matter. If these events happen before time, scientist seem to be suggesting that matter has always existed. They can only explain things based on their source of theories or beliefs which, for most, have not gone beyond the natural realm.

According to Genesis 1:1–2 of the Holy Bible, "In the beginning God created the heavens and the earth. And the earth was waste and void (formless and void or a waste and emptiness); and darkness was upon the face of the deep: and the Spirit of God moved upon the face of the waters." In Genesis 1, we get a slightly different account of how the earth was formed. In detail, it explains how God gave light, created the atmosphere, seasons, days, and years and separated the water from the land. Here, you do not have to have titles or degrees to understand how time and the earth was formed. The complexity of time has been presented so simply in the Holy Bible that some scientists dismiss its explanation as absurdities.

Time is normally associated with numbers, and that's because time is calculated and found in the order of everything. Order or commands is what holds everything we see in place. These commands or orders must come from somewhere or from someone; someone had to put instructions in these commands because nothing can't create something. Something has to come before everything else we see. Someone had to tell matter to compression and to explode. Bang! Can matter command itself, and does it have a mind of its own? Scientists skate around the acknowledgement of such an idea, but the only way to explain the unexplainable is to admit the existence of God. In our bodies are special instructions or commands called DNA that gives instructions to our bodies on how to function. Time is like DNA in that it is the synchronization of life by the creator to bring order to chaos and eventually bring understanding to purpose. We use watches, clocks, calendars, seasons, and the changing of days and nights to measure time, thereby bringing order to our lives. Time helps us manage everything that needs managing in our lives. We are called to be managers and good stewards over what God has given us, and God has given us time outside of eternity. Eternity is forever, but time is temporary. Everything that goes on in eternity never ends, but those things that go on in time have a determined end and a divine purpose. Because of time, we have change; but when time is up, everything stays the same which means what was, is, and will be happens in the same space. There is no time between past, present, and future. This concept extends beyond our full comprehension. It's called forever, and in our humanity, it is hard for us to understand something that will never end.

Time and the Generations

One Generation passeth away, and another generation cometh; But the earth abideth forever. (Ecclesiastes 1:4.)

Men shall come and go, but the earth shall remain. God has always had a plan for the earth, and after the day of judgement, it shall be renovated for the saints to live and reign on as it was intended. Here is a poetic expression, before judgement, of how generations come and go.

Anew

The Glory of the sky, the sun, faithfully comes up anew,
Shining brightly and awakening the earthly
greens that are wet of dew.
The chimes of the creatures of the air sing relentlessly—a
harmony that fills and flushes the mind,
Rest and peace that surpasses all understanding
are held in these moments of time.
The cool breeze of fresh air awakens the essence of all that exist,
Dormant is the new day awaiting to be lived in full,
wastefully by fools, a day they shall miss.
For time is the law at work in our bodies—growing
more and more precious each and every day,
As the children bloom as flowers in the spring, they remind
us of the frolicking joy missing because we no longer play.
An old man smiles while passing time rocking slowly in his chair,
Watching the world change around him,
rapidly it seems, into time he stares.
He allows his mind to take him to another but familiar place,
A place almost forgotten—a place before the wrinkles in his face.
He remembers the mornings as a lad—
when he once came out to play,

Standing in the dew—as an old man from the
porch watching him back then would say.
Young lad, enjoy the days of your youth:
enjoy the potential of each given day,
Watching you, son, I just noticed the sun setting on my
life, as I am, all of my memories are fading away.
Dim are my eyes that now struggle today
to see the newness of tomorrow,
Live each moment in such a way that you
have no regrets—avoid my sorrow.
Of growing old, most miserably alone, with nothing but these
walls that surrounds me in my heart and in my home,
Avoid wasting time pushing others away—until no one is left,
By all means do the things you've dreamt of;
sacrifice for others and not just for yourself.
Respect the old and give to the poor,
The road ahead circles back for all to endure.
Love everyone as loving yourself with all your heart,
We're one—the human race until death do we part.
In all you do, do it for the Creator because in the end this
is the only thing that matters—our purpose our call,
What is life but a moment, a breath of air, a vapor, and the wind
that comes and suddenly goes? And like that, It happens to us all.
I've warned you, young lad, you were told,
Fading back in, the lad—the old man now
realizes that it is he that is now old.
Searching his soul, grappling with his own mortality, he
watches the children, as he once did, draw near in their play,
Tears fall from his wrinkled eyes as he opens his mouth to say.
Please listen to an old man okay,
Time stands still for no man; the proper respect for
time is the beginning of success in all things.
Your tomorrow will be the result of how you live today.
Respect the old and give to the poor,
The road ahead circles back for all to endure.
Love everyone as loving yourself with all your heart,

We're one—the human race until death do we part.
In all you do, do it for the creator because in the end this
is the only thing that matters—our purpose our call,
What is life but a moment, a breath of air, a vapor, and the wind
that comes and suddenly goes? And like that, It happens to us all.
As the old saying goes "Once a man but twice a child,"
It's not until the end that we realize that our
time in life is only for but a little while.
Think of what I'm saying as giving you understanding
and a glimpse into an old man's mind,
Take what I've learned and be wiser today so you will have
no regrets and be counted faithful in the fullness of time.
Take these my last breaths and live your life Anew!

No one can reason with time because time is unreasonable. It can't be brought or swayed for favor or leniency. It moves forward indifferent with us or without us. Again, we see as depicted in this poem, there is nothing new under the sun; time is circular in that everything tends to end up where it started. From the dust of the earth we were formed, and to the dust of the earth we shall return. As spirit-beings with a purpose created, we were sent by the Father; and as spirit-beings, we shall someday soon return to the Father.

Life is a journey toward revelation and discovery. As time passes and age settles in, we tend to come to a better understanding of the value of the space between the events we experience. What is life but mere moments in time, the breath we breathe in and out, or a vapor of wind that comes and disappears? Men come and men go as time runs toward running out into eternity. At birth, we all are given a set amount of time to accomplish the purpose for which we were born for. Purpose (meaning) and time are married together to give birth to the plans of God, the creator, for the earth and humanity. It is imperative that we spend our time on purpose in order to accomplish the mission we were sent for. At some point in our lives, we will be able to see and understand how short of a time we have here on earth. As we stare our own mortality in the face, we begin to see how short of a time we have to do what we were meant to do.

I have observed that for some people, there is a point in which they welcome death, or so they say. Dying for them is not the issue, but it is how they might die that is the frightful thing. The thought of being alone, being in pain, being disabled, or being a burden on loved ones are all reason for not wanting to wait and see how things turn out. We must always remember that as long as we still have breath, there is a reason and a purpose yet to fulfill in us or through us. *One sure way to take the fear out of living is to get up on purpose and to live our lives on purpose.* It leaves little time to think about how we will die because we will be too busy living. We must maximize the time given us, and at the end of the day, we will look back and see the time that made up our lives was well spent. The mystery of time is revealed in our lives as it unfolds, and those who live life to the fullness ultimately learn its value and the mysterious part it plays in the plan of God. Time eventually reveals the meaning or purpose of everything.

Old age is a conundrum; it's a blessing to get there, but it's a struggle every day to be there. Age is simply time passed, and this age shall someday pass for us all. Time catches up with all of us; and when it does, things begin to go, fall, or slow down. Despite the fact that things begin to slow down, time seems to speed up. A month seems like a week; only those who have little time left know what I mean. The smell of flowers and the beauty of our world become more noticeable. Everything seems to become new again. The things that once lack value in our eyes all of sudden seem to take on a whole new meaning as if seeing things as a child for the first time; they become invaluable. Fame and money are no substitutes for true love, family, and time. Out of these three, time is the most valuable currency in our existence because we can find true love again, and if we lose family, we can start a new family. But *time is only possessed while we have it.* When time is gone, it can never be replaced. *We will never truly know the value of time until it becomes a memory.* When a man's life comes to an end, he sits and wonders as he is faced with death if his living really meant something; he wonders if his existence made a difference. It's a sorrowful end for those who wasted their lives, but for those who lived to make a difference transition as smoothly as the slow beautiful setting of the sun. Their final thought: *What a beautiful day it was*, as they fade into the hopes of a new day. A light as bright as a morning glare awaken them unto their reward, and that reward is to see Jesus, the Son, in all of His glory.

Selah 2: 1–44

1. Every man must leave his father, but his father or the essence of his father never leaves him.
2. Time is neither friend nor foe; it is indifferent to us all. It is only what it is, moments that add up and measures the width of our existence. When life is finished, time is the dash between our birth year and the year of our death. Years after we have gone, time will continue its nonbias path toward the fullness of its purpose.
3. Some people wonder how some people do it; the answer is daily.
4. The young may walk faster and see clearer, but the elders know the way because they have been there. Google Maps doesn't have anything on experience. The advantage of our youth is that we can listen and learn from someone who has already made all of the mistakes. This will save us time and help us go farther than the ones who came before us have gone.
5. Even the world's fastest man will someday slow down. The struggle of getting to the top is not as hard as staying on the top because one has to accept his or her own decline. We should never let our money, positions, titles, and achievements define us. If we allow them to define us, we will feel lost if they should ever be taken away from us. When we discover our purpose in life, these things do not matter because we realize that who we are is much more than these things.
6. We can't spend our whole life worrying about dying, nor can we spend our whole life worrying about living. Worrying causes us not to enjoy the moment.

7. As time catches up to us, it will someday demand our attention, and slowing down will no longer be an option.

8. Sometimes, a good cry is good for soul; but when we finish, we should get up and get back to it.

9. We should never spend all of our time making money that we forget to make memories; after all, memories last longer than money.

10. Walking in love leaves us vulnerable, but it is a walk worth the vulnerability. Marriage is a walk we have to take daily so that we won't forget or miss the beauty of it.

11. At age forty, I found myself between two worlds, holding on to the past and running forward toward the future. Torn within myself, I was in a place of wondering where I belong. I was in a place between the younger me and an older version of myself. The things I thought I knew, I found myself beginning to question. The things I thought I could do physically, I found out that there was a more prudent and less painful way to do them. This new me had to find his place in this rapidly changing world and body. At the midpoint, we tend to question our ability to champion life. We wonder if we can keep things up, and we fear the limitations age and time puts on us. The uncertainty of the future messes with our mind. *We spend most of our life trying to get there until one day, we wake up and realize we are there.* Then we wonder, *Do we have what it takes to stay there?* None of us remain the same. Time takes care of that. Life is always changing, and none of us were created to just stay the same. There is so much more in us to discover and to develop. This is the moment that I realized I needed a new vision for my life. In the cycle of life, we should go from mountaintop to mountaintop (living and driven by purpose) until in the end, we run out of mountains (time). This is the key to living a well-spent life. If we are in Christ, we should lean on the fact that He holds our tomorrow and just go along for the ride while trusting Him to bring us to a victorious end.

12. If we don't gradually change with the times, we will wake up one day and feel as though we have been asleep for ten years and awaken to a world we don't quite recognize or understand. It's possible to adapt to the changes around us without compromising our character and principles. The Word of God is timeless, and it applies to all seasons and all times.

13. The older we get, the more we start sounding like our parents. When we realize this, for the first time, we finally understand. In that moment, our parents go from knowing nothing to knowing more than we thought they knew.

14. We can only keep what we share with others. The things we share are stored up in an eternal bank where nothing can rob us of its benefits or credit to our lives.

15. Life begins and ends with a heartbeat, a sound that pumps life through our veins, a sound that is a part of the genius of our existence. It starts our internal clocks and continues until time winds us down. All clocks stop in time.

16. Some people are in a place where they are afraid to go forward, and they are afraid to go back. They are just stuck, pulled over on the side of the road of life waiting and watching others head to where they were going and come from where they have been. This place is a place of their own making, a place of comfort soon to turn into misery. Where will misery take them back or forward? Only time will reveal the end of their story. There is one thing that is clear here: fear gets you nowhere in life; try taking a turn down the road of faith. Where we end up is far better than stuck in the middle of nowhere, wondering what could have been. It's far better than just letting life happen to us than we grabbing ahold of life and living it to the fullest. Living in fear may seem safe, but this life ends in regret. In the recipe of a good life, faith is required. This road leads to a place where dreams become reality. We should stop watching the goings and comings of others, and we should

get on the road of faith and see that which awaits us. It is a journey worth taking and trip that is assured to end better.

17. I now know the struggle of the elderly; how do we cope when everything we have known and trusted start changing? The friends we once enjoyed are no more, and the places we once visited are now long gone. The things we once did our bodies happily reminds us to act our age. The things we thought we knew now leave us with questions. Everything we try to hold on to slips through our fingers as water through an opened hand. Now, we are left with the question of "Now what. What do I do? What can I still do? Where is my place in this world that has changed for me so much?" Answer: We must reinvent ourselves and discover new skills and interests. We must meet new friends and discover new places. Every human being has the ability to adapt if they just let go of the fear of the unknown and embrace the new journey before them. Life is a journey and an adventure. We must let go of the fear and live courageously to the glorious end. Without completely throwing out the old, we must be always willing to try something new. It is quite possible that we might like it.

18. In our youth, we can afford to take more risk; but as we age, our risks need to be more calculated and measured because we have less time to recover from mistakes.

19. Forgiveness is easy when we allow ourselves to forget. Rehearsing our pain only keeps the wound fresh. To forget requires the power of love that only comes from Jesus. The balm of love removes the scar and completely heals until the evidence of a past injury is no more. Love sees those that hurt us as victims to a common enemy. Love releases and keeps no record of their wrong. "Above all, love each other deeply, because love covers over a multitude of sins" (1 Peter 4:8). In our flesh, this is hard to do; but I thank God, by His grace, He forgives me and, according to Micah 7: 19, cast my sins into the depths of the sea. We

should always delight in mercy because, at some point, we all will need it.

20. Tired eyes always see things and situations in their worst light. Time and rest changes how we see things.

21. We should be careful not to be so stubborn at times that we become stupid.

22. At some point in life, our minds will be willing, but our body will say, "Oh no you don't!"

23. When we are in the middle of a storm, it is easy to see all of the darkness; but if we will just look up through the eye of the storm, we will see a peace that surpasses all understanding—His name is Jesus.

24. We must always honor our commitments because it tells everyone everything they need to know about us. Can we be trusted? Once trust is broken, it takes time to rebuild.

25. Life and death are in one breath; one takes life in and the other takes life out.

26. Time is so valuable that kings can't even afford it.

27. Jesus lived in such a way sinner wanted to hang around him. He walked in a way of pure love and wisdom. We always say we want to be like Jesus, so we have to ask ourselves, Do sinners want to hang out with us? Do sinners respect us because we are real or authentic? Does our presence carry conviction or condemnation? Are the words we speak full of power and faith? Does hypocrisy get in the way? Does self-righteous and religion get in the way? Does a lack of love for what God loves get in the way? It's something to think about! We are called to love! Love God, love righteousness, and love people.

28. The work we do today must someday be left for someone else to finish. What matters most on earth is what we leave behind.

29. Hope is simply having something to look forward to. One of the greatest gifts in life someone can give us is hope.

30. Time can only be captured in a memory or a photograph.

31. To what end do we exist? If not searched out, time shall reveal it; then to us we shall know.

32. We can run in place over time and never get anywhere, what makes the difference in our running is found in our decision to go somewhere.

33. If we want to know things others don't know, we must take the time to read the books others won't read.

34. We never have to teach anyone how to do what's wrong because it's in our nature, but we do have to teach others what's right.

35. People pay us for what we know and our time, and what we don't know, we will have to pay others for and their time.

36. Wasted time is wasted opportunity, and an unfocused life wastes valuable time.

37. The day we begin to doubt faith is the day we lose it, and when we reject God, we attract deception.

38. Some wounds are so deep that it takes generations to heal because the wounded get stuck in a cycle of reenacting their injuries.

39. When we are in a hurry, everybody and everything appears to move slow. If we would just slow down a little, everything around us would appear to speed up. Sometimes, we have to go slower in order to go faster.

40. Never is like always; they rarely exist. We should never say never, and we should be careful when we say always.

41. We should grow where we are planted because development and growth always take time. A premature transplant could mean the death of our dreams. We should examine the time and season that we are in so that we can judge the optimal time to make a move.

42. A seasoned man remains silent when he doesn't know something while a fool pretends to know.

43. The more we learn, the more we learn just how much we don't know. Knowledge is infinite, but our finite understanding is always limited to where we are in life.

44. At the end of earth's chapter, we are left only with a stone with our names carved in it. The remains of what used to be is all that's left to testify that we did exist on earth. We should live in such a way that more than just this testifies that we did exist.

CHAPTER 3

The Mastermind Behind Time

> And he said unto me, it is done. I am Alpha and Omega, the beginning and the end. I will give unto him that is athirst of the fountain of the water of life freely. (Revelation 21:6)

WHO IS THE MASTERMIND BEHIND the concept of time, and for what purpose? Who was here before the worlds began? Who interrupted eternity and set time into motion? Yes, time has a beginning; and when it becomes full, time as we know it shall end. But who says when it shall end? How is the mystery of our existence related to time? The arrow of time goes one way from start to finish, but is that really the end or the start of a new beginning? Why did time start, and why are our days measured by it? We know that within time, all things come to an end, but then what? That is the mystery that only those who have access beyond the boundaries of time know the full answer, yet separated by this great gulf between life and death, to us, the answers are not for them to give. The creator of time left us a revelation of the mystery of the things to come and the things beyond our time here on earth in the Holy Scriptures; it is a glimpse into the hidden things that shall someday, at the appointed time, be revealed. There is one thing that is for certain, whether we acknowledge it or not, before the beginning had an end, God was, and right now God is the mastermind behind time.

Father Time

As parents, if we could write the story of our children's lives, we would; I believe God, Yahweh the creator, has written the story of our lives, but He has given us a choice whether or not we want to live up to the story He has written for us. Everything in creation suggests this; it is evident that God knows His will but somehow saw it fit to entrust us with our own will. As all parents do, He desires that His will becomes our own. According to Isaiah 46:10, a book of prophecy in the Holy Bible, God stated that He declares the end from the beginning and from ancient times things that are not yet done. According to Genesis 1:1–5 of the Holy Bible, it states that "In the beginning God created the heavens and the earth, and that the earth was without form and void." It also states that "God divided the light from the darkness and called them night and day which became the first day." How He did it, whether it was a big bang or Him saying with a loud boom in an empty universe which echoes to this day, "Let there be light," God has stated that before anything He was. There is no beginning to God, and there will certainly never be an ending to God.

There is a void in every man designed to be filled with God, but instead we have filled that void with other things (gods) that will not satisfy. They have no ability to save, and during natural disasters, I've seen people carrying their gods out of the wreckage and flood waters. The creator needs no saving. He is not a figure in one's imagination, nor is He a figure that needs us to carry Him to higher ground. We did not create Him, for it was He who created us. If we create a god, as some have (false gods and idols), then in a sense, we become a god unto ourselves, coming up with our own truth as we go along. There is one truth; and there is one God, our creator and the creator of everything, Yahweh. Faith is how we experience Him on earth, and there is nothing more real than the reality of the mastermind (God) behind everything we see. After all, other gods rot and erode away through time while the creator God shall remain forever. He has simply always been, and He shall always be.

The Purpose of Time

According to Genesis 1:14 of the Holy Bible, "And God said, Let there be lights in the firmament of the heaven to divide the day from the night; and let them be for signs and for seasons, and for days, and years." God did all of this for a reason. Everything has a purpose, and that is always true when it comes to time and seasons. By observing the seasons, you will see that each season is unique in its characteristic and has a specific purpose. The start of a new season is what gets us ready for transition or change. We never just fall asleep in one season and then wake up in another season all of sudden. It is a gradual change facilitated by time. God, in his genus, gives us clues of the upcoming change which gives us time to adjust. We adjust by cleaning out our closets to put away winter clothing and replacing them with spring or summer clothing. We also change which crops or flowers we plant, and we can tell whether or not if it is time to plant or time to harvest. In the winter, there is less of a requirement to tend to our lawns, but come spring we know that a lot of attention will be required as the grass and weeds grow. Seasons alert us to timing of ecological events such as hurricanes, tornados, wildfires, flash floods, or droughts. Seasons change how we approach life. They are generally something that we can depend on when it comes to change.

There is much more to seasons than what we can sense, feel, or see. Seasons result from the earth's axis of rotation being tilted. Now, was the earth suspending in the universe tilted for the purpose of giving us seasons? I believe so because God seems to be very intentional about everything He does. Is it by chance that we, the earth that is, is positioned in the right place capable of sustaining life? Why is this? It is because the world did not create itself or formed by accident. God, the creator, created the world by bringing those things that where chaotic into order as a part of His master plan for humanity to serve His purposes. According to the Book of Genesis in the Holy Bible, God created the world and all that is in it. Now, for someone to create or make something, they generally always have to have a purpose in mind. What is the meaning behind time? Well, in order to accomplish anything, it is required to have both purpose and time.

We are not here by chance, but there is a culminating event awaiting us all, an event that God will declare that His masterpiece is finished, and every knee shall bow and every tongue will confess that He is King of kings and the Lord of lords.

The destiny of humanity is in the hands of God, but the destiny of an individual soul rests in the choice of that man. Since before the beginning, He had a plan or a vision for His creation. Time consists of the past, present, and the future. As depicted in the Holy Bible, God helps us to reflect by speaking to us of the past. He teaches us how to live by giving us insight on the present, and He warns and reveals to us of the things to come—our future. In all of this and in all that we go through in life, God is giving us time to repent and to allow Him to redeem us unto Himself. This is what time is about; it is the patience of God to give man chance after chance before justice and judgement have their way. We are all parts of a whole. Every event in life converges like pieces to a puzzle; in the end, we will get the full picture. We will see His masterpiece.

> Let us hear the conclusion of the whole matter: Fear God, and keep his commandments: for this is the whole duty of man. For God shall bring every work into judgment, with every secret thing, whether it be good, or whether it be evil. (Ecclesiastes 12:13–14)

The Mystery of Our Existence and Time

From the very beginning, God has been telling us what His plan for the end of time will be. His will, which is obedience, guarantees us life. It is the inheritance of the children of God. Through many men over many years in many places to many different people groups, God tells His story and our story. Through many characters throughout time, He unfolds scene by scene the revelation of the greatest story ever told. God is the author of life and a great author always creates with the end in mind.

God created man in His image, yet something altered that image. And that something was the influence of the evil one, Satan himself, to disobey God. We call it "the fall of man." I believe that when God saw Adam, like a mirror, He saw a reflection of Himself. I believe, still today, that the will of God is to see Himself in each of us. Man used his will or his choice to disobey God through the lens of pleasure which is the same lie being told until this day. Disobedience separated us from His likeness, but as believers who have accepted the Lord Jesus Christ as the lord of their lives, when God sees us, he sees the blood of His Son. He sees himself in us once again. He sees His image.

Life, the breath of God, was given by God to an empty form of man from the dust of the ground, but for what? To make man alive, and to truly be alive is to be conscious of the creator and His dream for us. He has numbered our days in time, and He desires to fulfill His purpose in us as we live the story of our lives each day. We are all a part of an even bigger story to play. God writes the script, and we play the parts He has written, or we choose to play our parts except out of character. God has a purpose for each day of our lives, yet humanity as a whole has been dead set on rewriting God's script by not obeying His commandments. Jesus obeyed the narrative that was written for Him unto death. Out of His sacrifice, the will of the Father was demonstrated. His will is that we die daily to the flesh and to ourselves so that we may be able to, through our obedience, play the part God has written for us. Ironically, God uses bad characters too to bring His story to fulfillment. It never ends well with them because their character always dies at the end of their story. He gives us a choice to accept or reject the part He has for us. *With us or without us the show must go on; we can either be a part of Him or apart from Him.*

> Remember the former things of old: for I am God, and there is none else; I am God, and there is none like me, declaring the end from the beginning, and from ancient times the things that are not yet done, saying, My counsel shall stand, and I will do all my pleasure: calling a ravenous bird from the east, the man that executeth

my counsel from a far country: yea, I have spoken it, I will also bring it to pass; I have purposed
it, I will also do it. (Isaiah 46:9–11)

God is serious about the fulfillment of this story. The statement God made "I will bring it to pass" implies that time will be required, but why? It is because this story is developing, and when everything comes into focus, the picture of a holy, merciful God will be unde-niably clear. When He does judge, no one will be able to say that He was not just. Time is moving us all to a day of reckoning, and this is the mystery of time. Every moment works together intentionally to facilitate the unveiling, revealing, and the unfolding of God's plan; and like time, no one, no force, or power can stop it.

One of the toughest things to do is to love someone who doesn't love us back. We can't make someone love us. Otherwise, it wouldn't be love at all because love is a gift (something that we give) and a choice. In the same manner that God chooses to love humanity, he gave us that same choice or free will to love Him back. With this will, we can choose to love God, or we can choose to reject Him. There is such irony in this because how can the created thing say no and reject its creator? It is not even natural for us not to acknowledge and live for God. In not doing so, I believe that a person has failed in their existing for we only exist for him and not for ourselves.

Time from the Beginning to the End and to a New Beginning

In the beginning, according to Genesis 1 in the Holy Bible, there was nothing but darkness on the face of the earth. It was God who gave it light, and according to Scripture, it is the separation of darkness and light by God that gave us the first day which is the start of time on earth as we know it. Here, we have proof that it was God who gave the earth and eventually humanity time. The time created by God came before everything else on earth. Before there was an atmosphere or sky, there was time. Before there was dry land, there was time. Before vegetation, plants, and fruit trees, there was time. Before seasons, days, and years, there was time (the act of separating darkness from light). Before the sun and moon (God was the light), there was time. Before the fish and the birds, there was time. Before the livestock, creeping things, and beast of the earth, there was time. Before us, there was time; and before time and anything else, there was God. It was God in and through time that gave us life. Without the light of God, pushing back the darkness, time on earth would not exist, and such is everything else. This truth still holds true today.

Before God created man, He provided everything man would need to have rulership and government over the earth. Since man was created in God's image, He was created to rule the earth just like God ruled heaven. God's will was and still is supposed to be done on earth as it is in heaven. In Adam and through Adam clothed in the glory of God before the fall, the garden of Eden had become a prototype of heaven or the kingdom of God. Now, why did God create a being that looked like him and a place set up for that being to rule as He ruled? Only God knows the full answer, but in my finite understanding, it seems to make sense that every Father wants a son—someone to see himself in. Nature gives us clues as we see that everything reproduces after its own kind. One seemingly could infer that this is just the very nature of God since it is found repeatedly in His creation. Now, this prototype of heaven and man, in the image of God, ruling the earth as depicted in Genesis (the beginning) and Revelation (the ending) is the original plan, the very foundation of our existence. God has not changed His plan; He just gave it time to develop.

God gave man dominion (rule/responsibility) over the earth; it was as a gift from a father to His children. Here is a modern-day illustration of the theme of what happen between God and man.

The Failure of a Son

A father by the name of Jim purchased his son, Adam, a new sports car like his because of how responsible his son had been by not going the way of his classmates drinking and carousing but working hard and managing his life responsibly. Jim tells Adam that the car is his but to be responsible and never drink and drive. He also told Adam not to allow anyone else to ride in the car except maybe his girlfriend, Eva. A guy named Lucius (means light) that Adam knew through Eva overheard their conversation as he worked in the yard by the tree next door. Adam took the keys, which represented authority, access, and responsibility, from his father and got in his car to pick up his girlfriend for the Friday night football game. Lucius approached Eva. They knew each other and had talked previously on several occasions. Lucius convinced Eva to get Adam to go to a party after the game.

After the game, they went to the party, but unknowingly Lucius had a sinister plan. While Adam was distracted, showing off his car and trying to fit in with everyone, Lucius, the yard boy, offered Eva a drink that was spiked with alcohol. After a few drinks, he convinced her to share some with Adam. Lucius told Eva to tell Adam that the drink would make him feel more confident and alive. Adam took one drink, then another, and another until eventually He was drunk. The image His father Jim had of him had begun to die. By this time, the jealousy yard boy, Lucius, told Eva that he wouldn't mind driving them home in the brand-new sports car. After all, his father told him not to drink and drive. Eva told Adam what Lucius said, and Adam consented. Lucius took the keys from Adam and drove them home to his delight, but he kept the car for the rest of the night. Lucius finally had the keys which gave him access and authority over what was given by the father to the son.

Adam stumbled into his house and ran to the bathroom. He closed the door and threw up all over the floor. By then, Jim was knocking at the bathroom door. Adam said, "Go away, Father. I'm a mess."

"What happened?" exclaimed Jim.

"I did what you told me to do—I didn't drink and drive."

"Who told you to say that?" asked Jim. "And how did you get home?"

You see, half the truth is still a lie. Jim finally entered the bathroom only to not recognize his son who was laying in his own vomit. "Son, I gave you the car because until now, you have shown me how responsible you are by staying away from anything that would hinder your good judgment. You reminded me of myself at your age. You were so responsible and diligent. Where are your keys, son?"

"I don't have them. Lucius, the yard boy, who drove me home has them. Eva got Lucius to bring us home safely."

"You could have called me, son. There is no excuse."

"It's not my fault," exclaimed the son. "The girl you trusted for me was the one who gave me the drink."

"Nevertheless," said the father, "I told you what not to do, and you knew better. I will tell Eva's father about her part in this as well. Because you have done this," said Jim, "you will walk, ride a bicycle, or ride the yellow school bus for the rest of your senior year in school."

In looking in the eyes of his father through the disappointment, for the first time, Adam sees himself. He now remembers the wrong turns he made that caused him to lose his way. He was drawn away by what was already in his heart—his own desires. It was these desires that silence the voice of his father; Eva was deceived, but he knowingly allowed himself to be led astray. As his father talked to him, he couldn't help but focus on one word, *son*. His father still called him son. He could see the love and disappointment of his father as he spoke to him. He never wants to disappoint his father ever again. He got up out of the mess he made and allowed his father to help him clean himself up. Jim gave him a robe to put on and told him to go to bed. As Adam turned to walk away, Jim called his name. Adam turned and looked with a tear in his eye; Jim said, "Son, I love you, and there is nothing you can do to change that." Standing in the grips of unconditional love, tears streamed down his face.

No more words were spoken that night. Jim, an off-duty police, changed clothes (put on flesh in the form of Jesus) and got in his truck and drove until he spotted the car he gave his son. It was filled with other drunk teenagers; Jim took the keys and told Lucius, who took the keys from his son, that his driving days were over, and indeed they were because Jim had him charged with grand theft auto, delinquency of juveniles, and DWI.

That's not how the story ends; the father took back the authority that the son gave away first, and then the father initiated a plan to restore his son which was something his son could not do in his own strength. The authority the father had in his right hand after the appointed time was eventually given back to the son. The son was now like his father in that he understood that with freedom came great responsibility. This is what our Father Yahweh did, is doing, and will do for those of us who surrender our hearts to Him.

This story started at the beginning of creation with Adam. God started time and gave it to Adam to manage all that he had given him; and even to this day, whether we realize it or not, we still use time to manage everything in our lives. We use it for this, but time also has another purpose attach to it. Our time belongs to the Lord, and it is taking us to the conclusion of Satan's, as well as man's, rebellion on earth. Time is taking us to the conclusion of the greatest story ever told—the story of life on earth. It is the force moving us toward being face to face with the will of God. This story is about a loving creator being committed to His creation and demonstrating unconditional love for the hope of reconciliation.

The state that humanity is in now will not be the state we shall remain in. According to Ecclesiastes 3:11, God has set eternity in the human heart, which is a God-given awareness that there is something more than our temporary stay in this world. This is the foundation on which we were built as spirit-beings sent to a material world. No matter how far we get away from our origin, our foundation will keep us longing for purpose and meaning while on earth. *At the end of things, we are always brought back to the beginning of things,* things that really matter and have eternal value. This is the circle of time and eternity in our hearts.

Selah 3:1–44

1. My son often comes to our room when he wakes up in the middle of the night. At night, I always close and lock our door which may be strange to some people; but to me, God forbid, if someone should ever break into our house, with a lock door, I would have time to react and respond to an intruder. A thief in the night will never catch me sleeping

and unprepared to correct his ways. Anyway, when my son comes boldly to our door and turns the knob, he expects the door to open; but when it doesn't, he stands there and cry. Sometimes, I open the door immediately, and sometimes, I wait to see what he will do; I test him. When he sees that the door will not open, he turns and sadly heads back to his room. My heart immediately wants to open the door for him. No good father wants their son shut off from him when their son so desperately calls for and needs him. When I do open the door, he jumps into my arms, clinching me tightly as if I had saved him from some awful fate.

This illustration reminds me of when we, as children of God, come to the Good Father with a problem. A locked door implies that someone or something is on the other side. Not having the correct key can determine when or if the door will open. Faith and persistence are master keys that can open any door, especially the Father's door. On the other side of a father's door, we know that everything that we have need of whether it's salvation, food, resources, protection, companionship, advise, or just a hug, it's there. We stand there and knock only to find that the door is not opening or our prayers are not answered when we want them to be answered. We stand at the door crying and complaining. Now, the Father hears us, yet he waits to see how we will respond to his delayed response. He tests our faithfulness and commitment in seeking Him. He tests us until our temptation to complain turns into a heart of gratitude and thanksgiving. Will we persist? Will we continue to complain? Will we doubt He is even there? Will we doubt His commitment and love for us? Will we give up and lose faith that the door will ever open? Will we faithfully wait on him?

All during this time, the Father's desire is to answer quickly. But in delaying, we get to learn something about ourselves, for he already knows the contents of our hearts. Faith has to be tested, or else it just becomes wishful thinking. Faith is an anchor that is unmoved by situations, circumstances, or problems. It moves us to act in confidence that we are not alone. My son's history or experience with his daddy's response to the door assures him that someway or somehow, the door will open if he just, knowing that his father hears him, remain faithful and wait on his father. The door may not open how or when he wants it to open, but nevertheless, it shall open. Good fathers love to save their children from whatever troubles them. God will unlock and open the door. In the meantime, we should "trust Him with all of our hearts, and lean not to our own understanding" (Proverb 3:5). He will never leave us to suffer in the dark alone. Having a loving Father is something to be thankful for.

2. A child who doesn't have a parent who believes in him or her is already at a disadvantage. Parents are the first people that will ever give their children confidence and a dream. The courage to reach for those dreams are communicated daily by the people that know them the most. Children are gardens that grow what's planted in them.

3. If our lives do not line up with the words we speak, our words lose its power in the lives of those who hear them.

4. When we cry, we are just releasing our pain. It's okay to let it go; it generally makes us all feel better.

5. God always does things for us we don't deserve. That's what love does.

6. Once we understand the kingdom of God, we will go back and sell everything that once had value to us because now we understand that we have found something more valuable in the kingdom.

7. We take choices lightly, but a choice is as old as forever and should always be taken seriously. There is always a consequence that follows a choice, so we should choose wisely.

8. In the circle of life, if we can learn what was done, we can understand what's coming.

9. Sometimes, to help is to just be there so someone doesn't feel alone. No words are needed.

10. Family is like a tree in an orchard of trees. We are all connected, yet from our tree, we know that we are not alone in the orchard of trees. From our tree, we have our roots; and from those roots, we grow and branch out. Oftentimes, during the storms of life, we feel the need to revisit our roots. Those roots are our strength, our foundation, our source, and our stability. As we revisit our roots, let us not forget that at the center of the orchard is a tree that is the source of everything. It is the root that we must revisit in order to understand the full essence of who we are, why we are, and what we are to do with the lives we have been given to grow in.

11. Trophies collect dust, and honors get forgotten; the only thing that will last are the people we invest in who, in turn, invest in others and so on.

12. Drugs are the forbidden fruit of the garden all over again. They steal our identity and reduce us to shame and demonic control. Once again deceived by our own hearts, we become a shell of who we once were.

13. Having faith doesn't make going through trials easy; it just makes what seems to be an impossible situation, a possible situation; it turns hopelessness to hope and fear into security and an assurance that everything is working together for good in the end.

14. Life without purpose is not life at all because life is more than just existing. There is reason for the time in which we have been given. One day, that time will run out, and then we must give an account.

15. Oh, that I may not walk the path of fools, but that I may embrace truth to the point that I always live it, to the point that it is more important to me than living because in the end, the truth will be the only thing that truly matters.

16. How come people who love to talk always try to talk to people who don't have the patience to be around people

who talk a lot? I just don't know, but I do know a person who listens more, learns more. *We should never miss a good opportunity to listen.* If only everyone knew that! Here are some clues: If someone looks off or moves slowly away from us while we are talking, it might be a sign we might need to let them go. If someone haven't said anything in ten minutes because they haven't had a chance, we might need to stop talking. On the phone, if we finally ask a question and get no response, that person has put the phone down because they knew we wouldn't miss them; it's a sign that we need to stop talking. If someone looks at their watch and walks us to the door, it's a sign we need to stop talking and get out. If someone next to us falls asleep in bed without saying goodnight, it's a sign we need to stop talking. If we always seem to say the wrong thing at the wrong time, it's a sign that we need to listen more. If the person we are talking to forgets what they were trying to tell us because we interrupted them, it's a sign we need to stop talking. If someone has to talk fast when they do get a chance to say something, it's a sign that we need to stop talking. If someone tells us that we talk too much, it's a clear sign that you…well, I'll let you finish this one because I have learned when to shut up! I believe we do God the same way; sometimes, we just need to sit quietly in His presence and let Him tell us what He want us to know.

17. We always learn more listening than talking because we already know everything we know. Only fools allow their tongue to go unbridled.

18. It's possible to say something and not say anything, and it is possible to say very little and say everything that needs to be said.

19. The past only lives on the breath we give it.

20. We walk by faith and not by sight. We have to keep the faith even when we don't see a change. We have to keep the faith in spite of a bad report. We have to keep the faith when everything within us tells us to give up. Faith not

only can change our situations, but it can change how we see our situations. It can change us for the situations. Faith is something worth holding on to because it can keep us from drowning in despair.

21. Wisdom is not always guaranteed with age; just ask any old fool. It's possible for people to know something, but somehow, they never get around to applying it.

22. How is it that we never have enough time, but there is always time to start over?

23. Starting over is not always a bad thing. It just might be a God thing.

24. What should we do when God has a different answer for our prayers than what we think it should be? Just trust him because he knows the beginning of everything to its very end!

25. Being late is a sign of mismanagement of our time, and if we mismanage one of the most important things in this life, more than likely, we will mismanagement other things in our lives. Success starts with the proper respect for time. We can give some people all the time they need, and they still, somehow, manage poorly to still be late.

26. Don't despise the small beginnings; before a redwood tree was a tree, it was a small seed. Its potential was hidden within. Now, in all of its glory that reaches to the heavens, it testifies that great things can come from small beginnings.

27. Self-imposed standards (discipline) is the key to unlocking potential. Steady vision is the road toward getting what we see and hope for. Faithfulness is the engine of success.

28. Faith is a response to what God has already done.

29. When everything gets quiet, we hear things that otherwise we would miss. The same is true in our own minds; we all need to get quiet within ourselves so we can hear the voice of truth over the static of this world.

30. Life: It is a number that can't quite be figured. It's just a wonder we must walk out in all of its complexities given to us by a creative genius whose name is God. In the end,

everything will make sense as we see the pieces of the puzzle come together.

31. It doesn't matter how smart we are if we don't fear the Lord. All the wisdom of the world will be subject to the wisdom of God.

32. One of the worst things someone can do to me is waste my time, for it is something that they can never repay.

33. If we need the praise of man to be okay with ourselves, we are only a conversation away from not being so okay.

34. Always remember that true love isn't based on conditions, but it is based on a commitment to die to ourselves for the sake of our commitment.

35. We can't love God until we know Him, and if we know Him, we know that He wants us to love others just as He loves us.

36. A plan is the only thing on earth that can manage time. It is through planning that we choose how to spend our time.

37. Timing is everything; we can do the right thing at the wrong time, and it be all wrong.

38. To waste time is to waste moments of life; life is not for wasting, but it is for the living. Time is not for waste, but it is for purpose.

39. Do you remember being born? I thought not, but we were not even considered alive until the doctor slapped us on our butts and made us cry. When life slaps us on our butts, it's okay to cry; it's proof that we are still alive.

40. History reveals time's impact.

41. Money loans us time to do more of what we dreamt of doing but had to work.

42. Everything that we experience in life is connected to the purpose of why we are experiencing it. Our journey in this life and the lessons that we learn are connected to an even greater purpose, and the moments that make up our lives are designed to bring us to that purpose. We can resist it, but then we begin to erase its meaning which causes everything in our lives to become meaningless. Life has a mean-

ing which is our hope, and once we accept it, we begin to truly live.

43. We can't have a relationship with God if we don't talk to Him, and God can't answer prayers we don't pray.

44. Opportunities are moments or windows in time; preparation gives us access, but the lack of preparation denies us passage.

CHAPTER 4

The Season of Uncertain Times

WHAT DO YOU DO WHEN the idea of home, which is ideally a safe place or a soft place to land, no longer exist? Such a place as this, more than likely, exist or once existed for us all. Such places as these never last because of the toll time and change inflict on them. There is one thing for certain in life, and that is change. I often think about my grandparents who are now gone and the places around their homes where I found solace and peace—a secure place that always welcomed me home, especially in times of distress. There are some places and times in life you wish that would never change that will never be considered gone. The reality of it all is that time is indifferent to preserving the places, moments, and even people that are dear to us. Now, as I drive by what used to be, I remember a time left behind; stored and preserved are the details of these times in the compartments of my mind. I am forever impacted by the places, people, and experiences. As the sun goes down on yesterday, I'm left with the harsh reality and realization that life does indeed go on with us or without us. Someday, as those before us, we shall all enter a place where time is no more for us, and everything that is becomes forever. *Through those who came before us, we live; but through us, they live on.* This poem below contains memories written to preserve moments of time experienced at the home of my grandparents. Memories are the only things naturally that can capture and preserve time, and once those memories are lost, those experiences and the people are lost to us forever. Here's to memories:

Along the Gravel Roads

There is a sense of normalcy that is no longer because we live
in a world teeming and inundated with uncertainties,
and the things that have taken our sense of security have caused
me to think about and long for what used to be—simplicity.
There was a place off of Highway 17 North that if
you sped by, you probably would overlook,
If you slowed down just a little, you would have seen
a small gravel driveway that led to an old wooden
house sitting and tucked away in a little nook.
I remember slinging the many different rocks one could find,
quite often that enjoyable scene replays in my mind.
For it is a peaceful time and a place that no longer exist,
it is a place of simplicity, now only a memory, I miss.
What once was is no longer there,
all grown up with weeds—no one to tend
and seemingly no one to care.
We store experiences we call memories through our
sense of hearing, taste, touch, sight, and smell,
Things we sense that are familiar have a way of carrying us
somehow to a place suspended in time, but only a shell.
Of what used to be; time brings all things to an appointed end,
The people, the places, and even the secrets held as burdens within.
As I stood gazing at the emptiness of what remained,
I encountered the undeniable smell of burning
wood—a smell that's always the same.
All of my senses became heighten, and all of a sudden,
experiences, some thought lost, came flooding in,
as I'm transported to what was, yet is no longer, the
somber look on my face changed into a silly grin.
I remembered the summer evenings of catching hundreds
of lightening bugs right before the cover of night,
a strange phenomenon as we put them in a
glass jar—oh the glory of their light.

I remembered being annoyed by the buzzing
sounds of a horde of bumble bees,
we knocked them all down with sticks and buried
them ceremoniously around the trees.
I remembered the grunt of those dumb swine as they fought over
the spoiled slop poured from a red chitterlings bucket in their pen,
they ate any and everything; It's no wonder some
people believe that eating pork is a sin.
I remembered some of the conversations had while
we sat on the butane tank in the shade.
Breakfast and dinner were always the best, but for lunch
oftentimes, we had Bologna or Salami sandwiches with Kool-Aid.
I remembered there always being something
to tear down, fix, or to build,
an old wooden house is where we lived, and in the morning,
you could literally see your breath from the chill.
I remembered the heaviness of the quilts on our beds,
in the winter, I became quite accustom to sleeping
with those quilts, made by hand, over my head.
I remembered seeing love in action as my grandma would
gather wood early in the morning to warm our day,
With all the heavy lifting and gathering, old wood heaters are not
controlled by the modernization of thermostats—the easy way.
I remembered waiting to hear the crackling
of a hot fire before I got out of bed,
I would often make the mistake of getting my pants too
close that when I moved, they would burn my leg.
In summer, during the heat of the night, I remember the
sound of mosquitoes humming around my head as if
blessing their food, which was me, before they bite,
You could hear the sound of mosquito spray guns
pumping, almost as a symphony of relief, every night.
I remember the orange water cooler with one cup for us all,
and the mysterious room behind the kitchen that I
would rush by, because of fear, in the long dark hall.
The secret things of my grandmother that room did keep,

it was just something about it that gave me the creeps.
I remembered the seemingly endless rotary kitchen wall phone,
you could use it in every room because the cord on it was so long.
Now, I don't remember something called the party line,
but what I'm told is that anyone could listen in
on private conversations at any time.
I remembered taking turns licking the spoon
and the old pink cake bowl,
Well, fighting over it most of the time; I don't
care how old I was, that never got old.
I remembered the cool crunch of country corn flakes
that satisfied a longing for something sweet,
it became a tradition with unknown origins and a
late-night treat that was always a joy to eat.
I remembered awaking to the smell of Bradley's
thick bacon that filled the room,
the sounds of grits popping and the mixing of homemade biscuits
were all telltale signs that breakfast would be ready soon.
Speaking of biscuits, I remembered the peach cobbler and
country fried chicken evenings while watching the Pistons and
the Bulls, tour of duty, lonesome dove, or the WWF fights,
we would also watch shows such as "Hey Haw," "Knight Rider,"
"Air Hawk," and "Dallas" which is how we spent most of our nights.
I remembered the Twilight Zone, a signal, that
would let us know that it was time for bed,
my grandfather, a war vet, would watch all the way until midnight
when the station would sign off playing the National anthem,
leaving only static as his salute descended from his head.
I remembered the one bathroom that everyone had to share, much
like my brother and I's bath water, today, I would not dare.
I remembered Night at the Apollo, a show
that came on late in the night,
in the morning, we watched "Phil Donahue"
and "The Prize Is Right."
I remembered the Young and the Restless which started our
seemingly long day filled with adventure and situations,

We played games like hide go seek, cops and robbers,
school, mommy and daddy, freeze tag, hop scotch,
and mud pies which all required imagination.
I remembered music from Motown records
or the gospel on the AM station,
We could relate to the music that seemed to be
much more meaningful for appreciation.
I remembered the rain hitting the tin roof and
being the cause for us all falling asleep,
That plus the roaring of cars speeding down the highway
all sounds, still to this day, that faithfully repeats.
I remembered berry patches and plum trees
as far as my little eyes could see,
we would pick and eat all day long, after all, they were free.
I remembered visitors stopping by to sit for a spell,
as we snuck to hear grown folks' business, nothing
that interesting as far as I could tell.
Someone died or someone was born,
someone gave a forecast of the weather while
the other talked about his corn.
I remembered Uncle Joe, SL, and Jesse pop, all
characters country kids, even today, would adore.
Uncle Joe was a one-legged barber which was
something I've never seen before.
SL, my grandma's brother, had a very distinctive laugh, and
his number one phrase was "man, what you talkin' 'bout."
He was a jolly old man no doubt.
Jesse Pop was mysterious in that he lived alone, and
no one knew much about him even to this day,
he would just hang around all the time with no place to be or no
place to go so we adopted him as part of the family you might say.
We would mess with him, and he would mess with us,
until he would get mad and make a fuss.
I remembered that anything that was built or
made was built and made by hand,

a garden or a smoke house were essential
part of living and that of the land.
I remembered washboards and clotheslines,
Now gone, these were things that were common once upon a time.
I remembered cane poles and fishing holes; time
that was never wasted but well spent,
we often took those days for granted but in
retrospect, I see how much they truly meant.
I remembered walking a quarter of a mile to Mr. Oliver
Coleman's convenient store to buy candy for a penny,
and for my grandpa, a coke, and a cinnamon roll,
You could buy more with less back then, and did I mention
Mr. Coleman's mouthwatering homemade burgers—
the best burgers I believe that have ever been sold.
I remembered the walk home throwing rocks along the way, going
to Mr. Coleman's store oftentimes was the highlight of our day.
Mr. Coleman loved to talk; there was no need to watch the
news for he would tell you all you needed to know and more,
It's amazing how he knew and had everything everyone
needed in that little country general store.
I remember the little white wooden Baptist church
and the sounds of the wooden floors as the people
stomped their feet and sung their hymns,
it was as if the building came alive, and we were transposed
to a different time or thrusted into another realm.
Every Sunday, my grandma wore a large hat,
She wasn't the only one because all of the mothers of the church
had one and together in white in the front corner, they all sat.
I remember the preacher winding up and letting go
of a sound that sent waves down every pew,
the people shouted back at him, you know
that sort thing the black Baptist do.
I remember the guest church going first through
the line in the back for a plate,

the longer the preacher preach, struggling it seems to caught
his breath, the more we could smell the fried chicken,
mustard green, corn bread, and my favorite, the cake.
I remember the sense of community, we all were so connected,
as a child, I didn't have many worries, I felt protected.
I remembered a time when one bathroom and
one car was enough; we didn't need much,
A television in every room and a personal phone for every
member of the family, who could have thought of such?
I remembered not having one dime, but we always
had everything that we needed and more,
no one ever told me nor did I know that we were considered poor.
Times were hard and times were tough,
but our family somehow someway had enough.
We didn't have much, but we had everything,
everything that truly mattered like love and each other,
things back then more valuable than they seemed.
I find myself years later with these same old rocks in my hand,
Some I'm sure I've touched or thrown before, the only
tangible things left of the memories of this land.
Few things in life last long as I've witnessed the time thus far unfold,
Unlike the highway of memories rushed by and soon forgotten,
we always seem to take in the moments down gravel roads.
Gravel roads to me, will always be the best roads.

As in all things such as darkness, light, life, and death, time separates; and it will eventually, in time here on earth, separate us from our memories.

When Everything Changes

There is one thing for certain in life, we can count on change to happen. The changes we are experiencing these days are happening so rapidly. There is little time to compare one day to the next before something else changes. Most of us are left longing for what used to be; but what used to be is, painfully, no longer there. We have entered a new season—a new era full of uncertainties. The year 2020 has been dubbed as one of the deadliest years on record. America, and even the world, has changed forever due to a pandemic called COVID-19 which has decimated families and left loved ones alone to die. Schools were shut down for months; and at the start of the following year, teachers and students were expected to return face to face to school buildings, not knowing whether or not it was safe to do so. The following letter was written to teachers for encouragement to face the many challenges of what I call the year of uncertainties:

> We all feel as though we are taking a test we didn't study for. Well, let me ease your mind; this test doesn't count. We are the baseline to something that has never been done to our knowledge before in this century. This is not just a challenge, but an opportunity to do something courageous and once again sacrificial. We have entered a season where there is no room for comfort nor time to get used to anything. If we slow down and ponder over the things we cannot change, we will get left behind for tomorrow is no longer a mirror of yesterday. In order to keep up, we must be willing and able to change in a moment's notice. We are all being stretched beyond points, just months ago, were inconceivable; the task and the responsible before us requires bending and could be injurious without flexibility. So, relax, breathe deeply, but remain focused and measured on what truly matters; *we all shall finish in a different place from where we started, and that my friend is progress and growth.* Let's come together in support of each other, and let the joy of the Lord and learning be our strength. There is no doubt that we will run a race worthy enough that the history books shall remember. We were

born for such a time as this! Which means that everything we need to face or pass this test of commitment, we already have. By the grace of God, the human spirit has always been resilient, so let's make the necessary adjustments in us and around us to position ourselves for success. How well our students adjust will be determined by the hope we communicate (perfect love cast out all fear). It will take Faith, and it will take courage. *This is our moment to overcome some of our greatest fears and live through some of our greatest challenges.* Encourage one another not to shrink back because of the fear of the unknown, but to plow through uncharted territory knowing that the only thing any of us can do is our best. Because of our Faith in the one who holds tomorrow, nothing shall be impossible for us to accomplish each given day.

No one would argue the fact that the year 2020 was a year we would rather forget. With lost jobs and lost loved ones, there were a lot of painful moments for a lot of people. Of course, we have experienced hard and devastating times before, but 2020 was a year like we had never seen before because of all of things that were happening all at once. Life for all of us seemed uncertain, and with our eyes wide open, hope for the future seemed unclear. Every part of the world seemed to be in turmoil; and America, at this time, leader of the free world, led the way in its confusion.

Much like the year 2001, which became a pivotal point that changed something in America forever. It revealed that we were entering into a new season in which the invincibility of America was shattered. The world saw America on her knees, and for the first time, many Americans born after the mid '80s saw just how vulnerable we were. The pride of the Americans, our intelligences and military might, blinded us to the fact that someone or some group would dare attack us on our soil. What's worse was in the manner in which it was done. According to History.com, on September 11, 2001, nineteen militants associated with the Islamic extremist group Al Qaeda hijacked four planes and carried out suicide attacks against strategic targets in the United States. Two thousand nine hundred and nighty-six people lost their lives, and years later, nearly ten thousand more were still affected due to contracting various forms of cancer from the inhaled debris. This indeed was a new day, a different type of warfare and a total disregard for innocent lives. America was literally shaken. The attack on America held our attention for a while, but before long, it was back to business as usual. Little did we know then that 9/11 was just the beginning of the season of uncertain times.

According to Julia Donheiser, the United States has spent at least $2.8 trillion on counterterrorism since 9/11; and according to the Watson institute for International and Public Affairs at Brown University, the total war-related costs which include the Pentagon's war fund, related spending at the state department, veterans care, and interest payments for military operations in Iraq, Syria, Afghanistan, and elsewhere estimated to be over 5 trillion dollars. About six years later, the US found themselves in a housing bubble (sub-prime or bad loans) that led to a recession and eventually, a huge increase to the national debt. The global markets also felt the impact of recession and went in a tailspin, resulting in bank failures all across Europe which led to a currency crisis. The world was on the brink of a catastrophic financial collapse; yet with certain actions, the economies of the world, including the United States, recovered. This opened up our eyes to just how interconnected we are and to just how vulnerable we all have become as a result of greed and mismanagement of our resources.

Historically, wars leave nations with struggling economics. During the emotional zeal of retaliation against our enemies, no one used this historical fact to balance revenue verse expenditures. The US-led coalition occupation of Iraq required major shifts in money and national resources to the military. It is obvious the reason for this spending was that Washington knew something that the American public did not know or that Washington had no foresight of the ramification of the fiscal decisions they were making. Issues such as inadequate investing in the economic infrastructure, the rapid rise of medical costs, pension costs of an aging population, sizable trade and budget deficits, and the stagnation of family incomes in the lower-economic groups were put on the back burner and seemingly ignored. The compounding of these issues started America down the road of fiscal irresponsibility. As of December 22, 2020, America's national debt is 27 trillion, which is up from the about 10 trillion dollars of debt we had just twelve years ago. It is projected to continue to soar seemingly with no end in sight. What will be the result of this mounting debt? Time will tell!

Wars and bad loans were not the only threats to our financial systems and national security. The world headlines were filled with upheavals and disasters such as hurricanes, tornadoes, mudslides, floods, wildfires, snowstorms, blizzards, tsunamis, and earthquakes between 2001–2020. These cost several trillion of dollars according to Wikipedia. According to the Daily Sundial, containing and the prevention of viruses have also been costly. Viruses such as West Nile virus (284 deaths), anthrax (5 deaths), SARS-CoV (774 deaths), mumps (E. coli and salmonella, 0 death), H1N1 virus (swine flu, 12,220 deaths worldwide), whooping cough (160,700 deaths worldwide), Ebola (3,956 worldwide and 1 in the US), Zika virus (0), and finally COVID-19 (3,000 a day) as of December 2020, have all contribute to the US's mounting debt. It is currently costing the US trillions of dollars to manage this last virus and to keep the economy afloat.

According to Prophecy News Watch (PNW), we experienced the worst global pandemic in 100 years with more than 20 million confirmed cases, and more than 350,000 deaths in the US along in 2020, we have witnessed the third worst economic downturn (6.9 as of October of 2020) since the Great Depression of the 1930s (unemployment rate of 24.9 percent in 1933) because of a national lockdown to slow the spread of COVID-19. This has led to massively long lines at food banks. At the same time, civil unrest erupted in major cities all over America because of social injustice which has resulted in the rise of violence and murders by about 37% in 57 big cities, and we had one of the wildest presidential elections in our history because of the polarizing issues we have allowed to divide us and cause us to fight continuously with one another. We are indeed in great and terrible times, but there have always been times that have pointed to the days in which we live today. The only difference is that today everything has intensified and all of the prophecies and world issues seem to be converging all at once. Something has definitely shifted because the world as we have known it doesn't seem to be the same.

Nothing New Under the Sun

We all, at some point, long for the things that used to be because they give us such comfort. There is nothing uncertain about those days and places it seems; we know them well because they are already behind us. It is when we think of the future, which is somewhat an unfamiliar place, the not knowing can be quite troubling. The reality of it all is that our world is what "we" make it and what we have made it. If we don't change, it won't change. In the words of King Solomon, one of the wises men who ever lived, "The thing that hath been, it is that which shall be; and that which is done is that which shall be done: and there is no *new* thing *under the sun.*" We live in a world of cycles in which everything repeats itself. In thinking about the tumultuous environment that has been created over culture, moral, political, and economic issues, much like many others, I have questioned whether or not we have ever seen times such as these in our nation. Much to my amazement, although before my time, there has indeed been a time in our nation such as the times of today, a time in which our nation was divided, and there was a sense of uncertainty about the future. In 1968, our nation was divided over the war in Vietnam, issues of race, issues of culture, and over issues of morality. Even in the music produced during this time (though released a few years later) were words that sounded distinctly familiar. The lyrics still, to this day, echo the sentiments of the heart of a struggling America, songs like Marvin Gaye's "What's Going on" (good question by the way).

Mother, mother
There's too many of you crying

71

Brother, brother, brother
There's far too many of you dying
You know we've got to find a way
To bring some lovin' here today, Ya
Father, father
We don't need to escalate
You see, war is not the answer
For only love can conquer hate
You know we've got to find a way
To bring some lovin' here today
Picket lines and picket signs
Don't punish me with brutality
Talk to me, so you can see
Oh, what's going on.

What's Going On

What's going on is a question that is going on in everyone's mind, and it is the topic of choice around most dinner tables these days.

Contrary to popular belief, the times we live in are not as unique as we may think. In 1968, the country was angry; people felt that the direction of the country was really at risk. Does this sound familiar yet? It was a bitter and contentious election year, considered to be the roughest in history, which involved Nixon, Humphrey, and Wallace (Wallace, a candidate that could get people angry and violent). This is the same year Dr. Martin Luther King Jr. was assassinated, the same year of the Olympics in which two black Olympians stood on a platform as champions and raised their fist (with a black glove on) to the sky during the national anthem not out of disrespect (according to them), but to protest racism and discrimination in the United States. John Carlos and Tommie Smith, because of their commitment to the struggle for equality and fair treatment, was banned from Olympic competition for life. Not much has changed; it sounds like the same old songs but with different singers.

The year of 1968 produced words, phrases, and situations such as anarchist, make America great, get rid of the electoral college, bias news, national convention riots, political tricks and finger pointing, close poll numbers, talks of constitutional crisis due to vote counts, premature declarations of the presidential winner, the greatest come back in history, and disbelief all of which echo the moments we now live in. After the bitter battle, something significant happened that gave all Americans a sense of achievement and reconnection. According to Wikipedia, "The *Apollo 8* became the first crewed spacecraft to leave low Earth orbit and the first to reach the Moon, orbit it, and return." The crew had a special message on December 24 for everyone who turned in that evening (historic numbers); Bill Anders said, "For all the people back on earth, In the beginning God created the heavens and the earth and the earth was without form and void and darkness was upon the face of the deep... Goodnight, good luck, Merry Christmas and God bless all of you on the good Earth." In that moment, the last week of 1968, hope for the future was restored. The following year, man did something that took a unified effort; man walked on the moon.

> For one priceless moment in the whole history of man, all the people on this Earth are truly one: one in their pride in what you have done, and one in our prayers that you will return safely to Earth." President Richard Nixon

Okay, what is your point? There is nothing new under the sun; we have the same issues and the same fight. Year 2020 took us, but it didn't take God by surprise. If anybody knows what's going on, He does. In spite of the partisan fighting, riots, protest, viruses, social distancing, racial tension, quarantines, economic distress, natural disasters, trade wars, rise in violent crimes and suicide, and the moral decay of our society, there is still hope! When the world gets darker, the light of Jesus will shine brighter. We, who believe, shall rise above the darkness. Don't be anxious! We survived then; and we, with the Lord's help, shall survive again. Look forward in hope for the new challenges to overcome and the better days that are yet to come. In the words of Bill Anders, "Bless all of you on the good Earth!"

Selah 4:1–44

1. Is there any end to bad news, sad news, fake news, pandemic news, divisive news, and partisan news? We are on the brink of some very concerning issues such as opening school without being sure of the ramifications of such a move, a vaccine rushed to market with questionable safety concerns, a very active hurricane season, possibly war with China, out-of-control violence in cities where children are being killed, Christian oppression and persecution, lies and more lies, economic concerns that will possibly lead to shortages locally and globally, job losses, an election that could lead to more civil unrest, and the internal erosion of everything American. Where is all of this headed? Times like these should take us to our knees (in prayer) and humble us, but all I see is the hearts of men becoming even more harder. How much more will it take for us to repent and draw closer to God? What is it going to take before our eyes are open? There is no more security in our bank accounts, where we live, how many guns we own, who we know, and the supplies we have stored up. *Natural things can't protect us from something that is spiritual.* As far as I can see, our only security can be only found in Jesus Christ. He is the only assurance we have for safety and victory in such times as these.

2. Fear not, but seek truth, for it shall be your guiding light in a world covered in darkness. When Jesus comes across the eastern sky, darkness will give way to His light. At the sight of him, all enemies of God will be defeated. God is not worried. He is not anxiously reacting. He is ruling. He is in control, and if you belong to Him, He is in control of your life. You have no need to worry because He is a good Father.

3. Doubt is the first step we take toward losing faith. Satan knows that if he can get us to doubt, that there is a short walk to our defeat. Let's be real today because the struggle is real. Have you ever felt like God failed you? Have you ever felt as though He either isn't listening or He can't hear you? Have the things you have hoped for never materialized or the answer you needed avoided you like the plague? Have you had a word spoken over your life years ago, and now it looks as though it won't come to pass? Have you made declarations, only to be mocked by those who heard them? Have you risked being a fool for Christ, and have you stood out on a limb only to anxiously wait for the miracle to show up? Have you applied the word, or so you thought, in a certain situation, but you didn't get results? Have you prayed the same prayer for years—you've stood on, held on to it, and even written it down—only to hear silence and have no change? Have you done everything you know to do only to feel as though God wasn't interested in your struggle? Have you thought to yourself, *Where is He, and why is He silent?* Well, I'm here to tell you that in the classroom of life, you are not alone! You see, when the test is given, everyone including the teacher is silent, and this is why you feel as though you are facing the test alone. *Now is not the time to teach or learn, but it's time to apply what you've learned.* Use the faithfulness you've developed; use the endurance you have built up; use the joy of your salvation for you know where your strength comes from; use and allow your weaknesses to be okay because you know, in your weaknesses, He is made strong; use your knowledge of the story of Daniel in the lion's den; refuse to deny God, and praise Him come what may; use the hope you have beyond the grave; use the firm foundation you have to trust a God who holds tomorrow in His hands. Use the time you have while you are waiting to continue to serve and sacrifice even when you feel as though you are the sacrifice; use your history with God to fuel your confidence in his ability

to bring you out of whatever you are in or to face whatever it is you must face; use the faith you have built up to believe that a seemingly impossible situation can give way to an "all things are possible" situation; use your knowledge of what Jesus did for you and take comfort in knowing your value to God; use the life he's given you to lay it down just as he did for us, for if you lose your life, you shall find it; and finally, use your cheat sheet; lift up your voice and praise him through the storm until you see the Son" shining again. Situations in your life does not dictate if God is still God. Your tears are always noted and are never ignored or forgotten. The race is not to the swift nor to the strong but to those who endure to the end. Always remember that though the teacher is silent, He is still in the room with us, and having Him in the room (our trial, our situation, or our circumstance) with us is enough. He will never leave nor forsake us, and in that we can trust. We must keep the faith no matter what; for the trials in this world is only for but a short time, and remember with that, faith there is eternal security.

4. How long must we waver between two opinions? Either we are for him, or we are against him. Either we love him, or we hate him. Either we accept him, or we reject him. Either we believe in him, or we dismiss him. Either he is Lord of all or not Lord at all. How long will time give of itself that we may have a chance to change and turn our devotion to the creator of all things? There comes a point that whatever we have confessed to believe, we must live it, hold on to it, and walk it out in the midst of our situation. There comes a point when the words we declared have to be more real to us than the air we breathe. At some point in life, we will be faced with situations no one (meaning man) can help us with. That's when we know that we truly have a problem. The grace of God is the only thing we can cling to; it is the only thing capable of holding us together and keeping us from falling apart. His grace will walk with

us in and through the fiery furnace; it will hide us in the lion's den, and it will help us cheat death out of its victory. What should we do when all of our "friends" have left us? What should we do when an addiction controls our lives, and everyone has walked away from us? What should we do when we find ourselves in so much trouble that even our mama can't get us out of? What should we do when we have raised our kids right, but they act as though they have no reference of Jesus? What should we do when the doctors have given us up? We should believe God when He said that His grace (His ability to do for us what we can't do on our own) is sufficient! We must believe even when we don't see any change. Just give thanks and believe! In time, we shall see the faithfulness our of God.

5. To be knocked down should bring us to our senses. To be knocked out only leaves us senseless. The first blow should be the only wake-up call we need to understand the situation we are in.

6. There is growth in the struggle; our strength comes from the things we have been fortunate to endure. The thing that gave David confidence to face Goliath was the battles he had already survived. Our problems may seem big, but the only thing we have to do is reach down and say, "God if you brought me through that, I know you will bring me through this." Our confidence should come from our history with God.

7. If we never look forward, we may lose sight of what's ahead. There is no future in the past; there is only history. Our future is ahead of us and living back there won't get us there. Our history is a place from which we are supposed to grow from.

8. Mapping our way in life keeps us off the roads that won't get us to where we are trying to go. Be intentional with each choice and step; for our reward is just up ahead. It takes the undisciplined man a lifetime to get there while it will take us just a few years.

9. Whether or not we carry the title of teacher, we are teaching someone something through our words, our attitudes, our actions, and our work ethics. We all impact lives every day and hopefully for good. This is why in the eyes of God, which should be in our eyes as well, everyone matters; and together, everyone doing their part, we can make a difference.

10. We only worry when we are not sure of the outcome of our situation. Faith gives us an assurance.

11. A great example of socialism—Venezuela 2019! A man has to pursue his own destiny and not sit back and allow the government to feed him. This mentality has left the people hungry and wanting.

12. How one sees himself determines where one sees himself, and where one sees himself determines how far one will go. What you see, you will believe; and what you believe, you will achieve or not achieve.

13. The world we create is the world we live in.

14. What good is tomorrow if you can't get through the day? What's needed to get through the day is hope that tomorrow shall be better.

15. Faith is not reason, but it goes beyond reason. Reasoning is with the mind, but faith is with the heart.

16. Words are the most powerful things in the universe. In the absence of everything, God spoke, "Let there be light and it was and so on." Words are like seeds; the type of seeds you plant will produce after its own kind. There are instructions in our seeds or words to produce what's spoken or planted. We must choose our words carefully because what we say is what we shall have.

17. We should never depend on the praise of man to know who we are. For if we do so, we may never find ourselves.

18. At some point in life, we will question everything that we have ever known in life. The very ground underneath our feet will shift, and we will feel as though everything we have that is stable in life will show signs of falling apart. The

answer to all of this is found in the foundation of every-thing else around us changing through the vicissitudes of life. We ourselves, in some aspects, will change; yet year after year, the truth will remain. We should hold fast to the truth, and in doing so, we will not lose ourselves or suffer ourselves to be lost.

19. The consequences of some choices save their bite until the end.

20. Dehumanization of individuals starts at ignoring the sanity of life. This is how the institutions of slavery, the Rwandan genocide, and what happened to the Jews were justified. Not seeing individuals as God sees them gives us a distorted view of what a person really is which is a spirit-being made in the image of God sent to the earth for a purpose—His purpose. This spirit-being at birth is given a guardian angel or protector; this guardian angel is called a parent. To not protect a child is an unnatural thing to do, and this could easily happen if a person is led to believe that life begins at birth. If God is the giver of life, which takes place at con-ception according to Scripture, who or what could make a person think that it is okay to take life to satisfy their own ideological belief? That's something to think about! The devaluing of any life (the old or the unborn) leads to the devaluing of all life.

21. Life is tough, but it is worth the fight living. Some people fight for each breath, and they survive the night barely mak-ing it to the next day, only to still be surrounded by failure, hardship, and disappointment. Yet from a perspective in Christ, failure is just a platform to build from. Hardship is just a tool used to develop character and strength, and disappointments are just delays to an appointed time for breakthrough. The beauty of each given day is that it is a new start and a chance to reach for better and brighter days. There is hope wrapped up in each new day. Rejoice and be glad in it for this is a day that the Lord has made.

22. Why a heartbeat? A heartbeat is the sound that lets everybody know that somebody is home; the heart is the organ that forces life through the body. It gives everything the body needs to function in the time given by God to fulfill its purpose. The value of human life is what we place on it. The sound of life is first heard only by those who silence themselves long enough to hear the cries of justice and mercy, and lastly, it's heard by those who can hear their own hearts.

23. Where, how, when, to whom, and under what circumstances we were born all play a significant part in the meaning and purpose of our existence. No one is an accident, and we certainly can't stand in the place of God and correct what we feel is a mistake. Unless we are God, we can't see the big picture, and the significance of the role each individual will play in the complexity of this ingenious idea called life. No one is just material waste because God is not wasteful. He has required us to be good stewards over what he has given us; it is our duty to protect the sanctity of life. Every life has value and can be used according to His plan. We are all connected by a common cord in which we need each other to become our best selves. How many of us are missing and are absent from the part we were to play? I'm told countless millions.

24. To take a life because one feels as though he or she has a right to is a deception that takes root in an individual's void of the understanding of spiritual things. This demand for the freedom to terminate a pregnancy because it is a woman's prerogative only opens up an individual or nation who sanctions this sin to judgment because though the unborn can't speak, their blood testify of the evil that has been dealt to them. The blood spilled remains long after the unborn has been disposed of. The blood or life force will forever be a stain and a reminder of what was lost. On the day of judgement, this blood shall be there, and the only thing

that will satisfy justice for the spilling of innocent blood is the blood of Jesus applied to a repentant soul.

25. The answer to what's wrong with the world starts at home.

26. In the spirit, the earth is shaking. There is a cry for justice. A river of blood is bearing witness to the sins of the protectors who have failed by placing their will over the will to live of others. Some are godless and merciless while others are just blinded by the ignorance of darkness. The light of revelation is all they need to turn their hearts and the wrath of God that is soon to visit the nations of the earth that sacrifice their children to the God of self.

27. When blood is shed, blood is the only price that will satisfy the scales of justice. Sin required our life, but Jesus paid the price so we wouldn't have to. It is because of Him we have life and that eternally. We had no hope because of the sins of our fathers even before we were born, but Jesus protected us and gave us a chance at life. Injustice (sin or executing that which is wrong) attracts judgement. Justice shall not sleep forever. That which is wrong shall be made right. We must choose life before it's too late.

28. To survive and win the race of a 100 million sperm cells and not receive the reward of life is a tragedy, conceived as a natural winner but losing at the hands of destiny killers, ripped from a place designed for their development, growth, and protection, never to realize their potential nor to fulfill the life and assignment given to them by the creator. Who will speak up for those who have no voice? Who will stand up for righteousness and the sanctity of life? Who will protect and value the greatest gift we all have been given—life? Who will give up their life to save another? That's love, and not a political view!

29. Trouble comes to destroy the lie of our own independence. Life is a few days and is full of trouble. Never forget the truth of our dependency on God. Troubles in life are natural, and they have assigned to them time. Each season has its own challenges, but the peace that surpasses all under-

standing in the midst of those challenges is supernatural or outside of anything nature in the realm of time.

30. We can't blame God for the things that take place on earth. He gave the earth to us. It has been our responsibility, and as a result of us not assuming that responsibility, the earth and the things that go on in the earth "is what it is." So, before we point our fingers to the sky, remember that there are three fingers that point back at us. The wrong we see in the earth today is the wrong over time we have allowed.

31. We never fully know the gift of a given day until there are not many more left.

32. When time says it is time, no matter what we are doing or who we are, it is time to go home.

33. Death or living in the end-times shouldn't be a scary thing for believers in Christ. There is a reason He is called the savior; He will save us from the wrath and judgement that is coming to the earth. Death no longer has a sting nor can tribulation touch those who belongs to the bridegroom. True believers should be just as excited as a bride on her wedding day! All are invited, but the question we all will answer in our living is, will we attend, or will we be left behind?

34. There is a deception to sin; it's worse than it looks. The doors we allow to open today will be the path we will take later.

35. If someone you say you love is running full speed toward a cliff in darkness, would you warn them to stop, or will you say, "Well if that's the way they want to live. That's their life." Which is love? The wounds of a brother can be trusted. We are our brother's keeper; it is our business to get in their business. This is the original expression of minding your own business.

36. Worrying is like a treadmill; it wears us out and gets us nowhere.

37. Pornography, whether participating in it by producing it or to participating by watching it, is rooted in self-hatred. It is

a bondage that is self-inflicted, and like a drug, it enslaves its captives with the purpose of destroying the image or identity of God they were created in. A cry for love and identity is the cry of the fatherless who are trapped in a life-style that promises what they are missing, but it just leaves them emptier and more ashamed. To watch this perversion keeps those who produce it, somebody's daughter or son, enslaved. We can't enslave others and not become a slave ourselves. This self-hatred or perversion begets more hate that literally changes the reality of what's wrong and right in one's mind. Our image or value is diminished as we participate in acts that is the opposite of love. For those of us who struggle, we must allow ourselves to be accountable to someone (no late-night internet surfing; give up passwords and subscriptions; report your progress to a trusted friend; confess your sin; get professional help if necessary). Also, marriage won't cure this addiction; only the power of the Holy Spirit and the fear of the Lord can subdue this desire. By freeing ourselves of this secret sin that is destroying families, ministries, communities, and producing those who prey upon the innocent amongst us—children—we free so many others.

38. The normalization of perversion in our society is not just the world's problem, but it is all of our problem. A nation that changes its laws to support immorality gives birth to a misguided generation, and the blood of their folly will be forever a stain on the land. Justice in the form of judgment will be a price our children will pay. For it is our responsibility to ensure that the next generation knows truth and is left in a position to prosper.

39. Everything works fine until it doesn't.

40. Our appetite can sustain us or, if we let it, destroy us.

41. It is okay to keep our head in the clouds but never let our feet leave the ground. We should always stay in touch with the reality of where we are.

42. The roads of life do not always take us where we want to go, but they take us where we need to go. Development is not always easy but a necessary part of our growth.

43. History has taught us that people will justify the devaluing or mistreatment of others by claiming they have no souls. Reducing some to mere animals or tissues, in the twisted minds of some, makes brutal acts toward them justifiable. They divorce all consciousness of what is repugnant to God. Their own way is the way that leads to their own destruction.

44. We are made in the image of God. We were created to be a mirror image of the creator of heaven and earth. When God looks at us, He expects to see himself. When He hears our conversations, He expects to hear His voice. When God observes sickness, He expects us to speak to it and take authority over it. When God is moved by the needs of the poor, He expects to see His hands in the earth reaching out. When God is grieved by the hopelessness of the bound, He expects His light in us to walk into the darkness, and those who are blind to gain their sight which is their freedom. When God senses the fear of a crippled world, He expects the carriers of faith to arise and spread hope (the gospel, the good news). When God forgave sins through the sacrificing of His Son, Jesus, He expects to see a people quick to forgive. He expects a sacrifice. God expects to see Himself in the earth through His sons and daughters. We are His ambassadors or seeds in the earth from His kingdom. God's goal was, is, and will always be to colonize the earth to resemble His kingdom that His will shall be done on earth as it is in heaven, and soon it shall be. Our identity is in God; it's not in our race, party affiliation, or denominations. We matter because He matters and because of what Jesus did for us all. It is the evidence to those in the spiritual realm and in this realm of our value. The creator of all things submitted himself to this life and gave His life to save ours. Man's assessment can't calculate our worth to God, so when we

see ourselves in a mirror or when others see us, can they see God? When they hear our voice or our conversations, can they sense or feel God? Do they recognize His love in us for them? Can they see God in the earth through us? The correct answers to these questions are the only thing that can bring about change in the wicked hearts of men. Anything else is just foolishness and a waste of time. We, who are reflections of the light of God in a dark world, must occupy and influence the territory given to us until the return of King of kings and Lord of lord's to set up His kingdom on earth. If you truly belong to God, everyone will see a resemblance. *There is only one division we should be concerned about that will forever divide us: it is whether we belong to the Father or not. This is the only thing that truly matters!* We should take an honest look in the mirror and see what we see. What we want others to see in us (for example, value) we must first see in ourselves. Do we see the Father? Do we see His Son and His love for us? If not, as long as there is still time (which, at some point, will run out), there is still hope for us! We must seek Him while He may be found; then and only then will we find our true identity. Then and only then will we understand (no need to fight, argue, point fingers, or choose sides) what truly matters.

CHAPTER 5

The Season of Justice:
Out of touch

"It's A Wonderful Life"

MOST OF US ARE FAMILIAR with the popular Christmas story of "It's A Wonderful Life." It's a story of a young man, George Bailey, who aspired to leave his hometown to venture into the world to make a name and a fortune for himself. His dreams were cut short due a sense of responsibility to his family. His father had become ill, and he was next in line as the man of the house. He felt compelled to live up to the expectations that was placed on him all of his life. "Good old George will come through for us." You see, the people of the town needed his father's business to continue because it was a lifeline for the poor man.

Although George lived in a small town, he was a big man to most people because of his personality and his natural ability to serve and lead people. His gifts had somehow trapped him in the place he had so longed to escape. He was as a lion in a cage, meant to be king of the jungle yet unable to rule his own destiny. Every move or attempt to get free he made only entangled him even further. He watched his friends go off and do the very things he wanted to do; they had made their mark on the world. He, on the other hand, sacrificed himself daily, watching the years pass by as all of his plans and dreams slipped away. Even though he had a genuine love for the people, he was frustrated and felt as though he wasn't living up to his full potential. He had inherited a burden that was not of his own, and seemingly, to him, was left with nothing of significance (according to his understanding) to show for his life.

Sure, he was rich in friends which later in life he learned to appreciate; but before he came to this realization, his life was not turning out the way he had hoped. In fact, after diving into life to save others, he found himself drowning, seemingly, alone with no one to save him. He began to lose hope; and in the process, somehow, he lost his drive and passion for life. He felt as though he was worth more dead than alive. He felt as if life robbed him of every opportunity to get ahead. He felt like a failure, and he no longer wanted the gift that made him who he was. In the pot of life, every time he tried to get out, there was always someone there to remind him of the lid that was over his head. After years of this, he felt as though his life didn't matter; and at this point, he was not aware of the impact his life had made to so many. The vicissitudes of life left him at rock bottom, but divine intervention helped him to understand what truly made life wonderful. He had character, integrity, faithfulness, trust, good friends, family, and last but not least, God, all of which would stand the test of time far longer than any worldly pursuits of grander.

Through the miracle of love which never fails, life had finally become more than the emptiness of longing to be rather than just being what and where God had called him to be. Time takes us on this journey, maybe not the one we've hoped to be on, but it's up to us to make the best of each opportunity and grow from those experiences whether good or bad. A wonderful life is determined by what we are leaving behind that will positively impact others throughout time. "Each man's life touches another man's life." A wonderful life is a life of meaning and fulfilled purpose no matter how big or how small. Riches are found in relationships and not the things we so often foolishly chase. A person who is okay with who they are and what they have been called to has learned something that some people will spend a lifetime learning, and then it's too late. You see, *it's possible to have everything and not have anything, and it is also possible to have very little but have everything that truly matters.* What matters to God is what truly matter in life, and what truly matters to God is people. If we all matter to God, we all should matter to each other. How much people matter to us or how much we value them is communicated through our actions toward them.

George Bailey lived to see how the people he gave his life for valued and appreciated the impact he had on their lives. As they poured out their love for him in his time of need, which was good to see, but he still didn't lose sight of the lesson that he had learned. George now understood that he and what he did for others (love and sacrifice) in this life mattered to God, and in the end, that's all that truly matters. "When a man's ways please the Lord, he maketh even his enemies to be at peace with him." (Proverbs 16:7). In the end, George learned from his angel Clarence that "No man is a failure who has friends." George discovered that day just how rich he was.

The thing that would make life wonderful for us all is to have a sense of community and being that proverbial "brother's keeper" that we often fail to be. It means looking out for each other and not holding on to past wrongs. It means being accountable for our own actions and not being so quick to blames others. It means forgiving one another and making ever attempt to understand each other. It means meeting each other halfway instead of always demanding our own way. It means reaching out instead of only being consumed with ourselves and our own. Life is much better when we share it with one another. In the good times, we should rejoice and celebrate with each other; and in the bad times, we should come together to help and comfort one another.

The sad thing is that the very things that should bring us together can be used by evil influences to tear us apart. Our society has been inundated with divisive ideology and rhetoric because of the painful memories of injustices centuries ago that has inflicted a festering wound so deep that it stirs up painful emotions every time injustices occurs. America was envisioned by my white brothers; but it was off the backs of slaves America was built, became rich, and eventually found her conscience. These facts still haunt most people of color. To some of us, America will never be able to repay the contributions of the African brought to her shores. The offense of our ancestors' dehumanization seems to still plague the black man in society even today. The deposits of the blood of Africans were the price that was paid in order to birth this great country, but the miscarriage of being treated as second-class citizens makes the sacrifice seem to be an insult. Such a sacrifice should be an honor; but against our will, raped of freedom, it was and still is our disgrace. These facts, in conjunction with the disenfranchisement most black people feel, even today, stirs up anger which, unfortunately, in some people, can become an anger beyond reason. The response to injustice played out in the streets of our communities is the built-up anger of feeling helpless to change ones standing and acceptance as an equal in society even after all of these years. Hate is still the reason why we feel as though we can't breathe, and the reason why we are dying stems from being hated, as well as our own self-hate.

There are no easy answers or quick solutions to an issue so deeply rooted in all of our hearts. We have to learn to forgive; and let God, and not we ourselves, be the judge of the injustice of slavery and bigotry. The sins of a nation and of a people will be judge not by us but by God alone—the righteous judge. In our struggle to not only to be free bodily but also in our minds, we, descendants of Africans, must not forget our responsibility in conducting ourselves in such way that it compels others to not be able to deny us our God-given right to dignity and respect. This problem between my white brothers and my black brothers is very deep, and without the unconditional love of God found in forgiveness and understanding, some of us will continue to be blinded by our own ignorance until we are drowned in our own hate. If we expect God to forgive and bless us, we must acknowledge and forgive the past, find mutual respect, and love in the present and embrace and value each other as brothers and sisters in the future.

Where Division Starts

Where there is a difference, there is always a possibility of division. The forces of darkness know that there is power in unity, so it is their full-time job to cause division based on information they have gather from us. God made us different and made our differences to fit together for one purpose, His purpose. We are different mainly because of our experiences, yet at the core of our being, we are the same. We have the same hurts, pains, issues, fears, hopes, dreams, and the same creator. It is when we see situations through the filter of personal pain, we tend to judge situations and each other unjustly. Clouded by preconceived notions, facts, and truth lose their power to even matter because somehow, we override reason and form the narrative that aligns with ever bad experience we have had. At this point, no one can tell us otherwise. We see only evil as we stereotype those we have had bad experiences with, and we are not even convicted about not acknowledging the full truth of the matter. We immediately take side based on color and not the content of the situation. Finding someone to blame temporarily numbs the pain, but this pain causes us, at times, to become irrational in our thinking. Against closed ears, facts become vain to bitter hearts; and ignorance from this continues to divide, destroy, produce fear, and tear everything apart.

There is no doubt that there is a problem with our justice system, but our goal as men should be not to do anything to become a part of that system. That effort must begin at home, with parents of all races raising their children in the way they should go and teaching them the love that God has for everyone. Parents, as being the first teacher of a child, should teach their children to have respect for authority and the fear (reverence) of the Lord. Is this "unjust" system, as some believe, the cause of the problem or the result of the problem? Is it the legacy or curse of slavery? Is it poverty in which all sort of issues come out of? Is it a breakdown in the family structure? Is it just pure hatred for those who are different from us, or is it all of the above?

We live in a culture in which a black child who is more interested in his studies rather than being consumed with sports is accused of acting white. We live in a culture in which a black child who develops his vocabulary and becomes articulate is also accused as acting white. This leads me to my next question; why is acting black always seem to be attributed to something non-productive or non-intellectual in our society? This seems engrained and communicated in the culture beliefs of society and the poorest black communities. Is this how we characterize or see ourselves? Is this something we have told ourselves based on our own beliefs, or is this something we has been taught through our interaction with society? On the other hand, my white brother, in an effort to be cool or fit in with black people, pulls his pants down, curses, and speak broken English (slang) all in an effort to act black. Who told him that acting like this would get him accepted in the black community? Who educated him on being black? Did he learn by watching us call a woman female cows and garden tools, or did he learn it from his "supposedly" racist parents?

Something is not quite adding up here! Could it be that we are just as responsible for our own plight than anyone we could ever blame? There is indeed a crisis in the black community; and it is much more than drugs, crime, education, poverty, and police. The crisis, without regards of individuals but collectively, in the black community is identity. All the other ills of the black man stem from this. Who am I, and where is my place in this world? An answer to these questions will be the answer to our problems. No longer will we have to demand from others to acknowledge the fact that we too matter. Once we know it, it will be automatically known.

Poverty, Crime, Brutality, and Authority

According to the Bureau for Justice statistics, people living in poverty are twice as likely to commit a violent crime than people not living in poverty regardless of race. According to an article written by Troy L. Smith, four hundred years of systematic racism is the reason the poverty rate is more than twice as high in black Americans than white. From a balanced perspective, systematic racism is partly the cause of poverty in the African American community, but the other part is personal responsibility on the part of individuals in the African American community. Proof of this is found in the fact that not all African Americans are poor, and not all white Americans are rich. Poverty and crime are not isolated to one race. The term *black* on *black crime* has been wildly used by both white and black people. It is generally used to deflect away from police brutality. Many truly feel as though black on black crime is more of a problem than police brutality. According to statistics, both of them are a problem and possibly one being a contributing cause of the other. Crime in the black community generally is black on black, but the same can be said in the white community. There is black on black crime; but there is also white on white, white on black, black on white, and so on. What does statics from the US Department of Justice say about white on white, black on black, black on white, and white on black crime? The rates of white-on-white and black-on-black homicides are similar and remain within ten percentage points of each other, around 80 percent and 90 percent, respectively. Likewise, rates of black-on-white and white-on-black homicide remain within eight percentage points of each other, at around 16 percent and 8 percent. This suggests that each group is killing themselves more than they are killing each other, and there is not much difference at the rate in which they are doing.

Is police brutality a cause of the problem or the result of the problem? Are we serious about defunding or dissolving the police force? Seriously! Who do we think will suffer the most from this radical ideology (to put it nicely)? We all will (black, white, Hispanic, and Asian people alike)! Shootings and crime would become more of a serious problem than they already are. According to a "*USA Today*" report by Camille Caldera (September 29, 2020), America does have a problem; but in my opinion, it is only symptoms of an even deeper issue. According to the fact-checking data published in this report, the US Department of Justice, Bureau of Justice states based on population (about 60.1 percent white vs. 12.2 percent black),

> Police kill black people at disproportionate rates. The fatality rate was 2.8 times higher among black victims than white victims. Black men are about 2.5 times (Black women 1.4 times) more likely to be killed by the police over the course of their lifetime than white men. Now why is this? Is it because of hate (from both sides),

fear (from both sides), aggressive behavior (from both sides), non-compliance, stereotypes, or a high ratio of white cops policing black people? It could be one of these or a combination of these. *Again, according to this data, police kill Black people at disproportionate and much higher rates than they kill their white counterparts.*

Now, if this data from the US Department of Justice is accurate, this is indeed a complex problem, and it seems to me that there needs to be reform in police departments, as well as "parental departments." *The weeds coming up today are the seeds that were planted in all of our children years ago.* The surface of our problems is just a sign of an even deeper problem rooted in the hearts of men. Our true enemy would have us to believe that the issue is color, but the enemy we all fight is invisible. *The real issue is not skin, but it is sin.*

Power and authority are like electricity. If used properly, it benefits us; but if used improperly, it can kill us. Law is the established standard of proper conduct derived from the consciousness of that which is considered right. Laws and power are given to those who assume the authority established by the people which is a system of order sanctioned by God. When this order is interrupted, the power of law is lifted, and as a result, lawlessness erupts. Authority is for the service and the safety of the people and a deterrence from lawlessness. When that authority is diminished, the forces of rebellion give freedom to the destructive will of man to submit only to himself. In other words, without law (a mirror) man is unable to measure his depravity which, more than likely, will lead to an unconsciousness of God and nothing good. Man, in a sense, becomes his own god judging his own conduct as he sees fit. I caution us all not to go down this road.

We all must learn to respect authority, and if that authority is corrupt, we must prayerfully demand and initiate the established order for change. Good authority should never be forgotten and should always be distinguished from the bad. Those who have been given the authority to protect and serve are just as humanly flawed as we are, yet as we all do, they need accountability. *It is in the absence of accountability that a culture of corruption is born.* Our humanity inherently gives law purpose, and those who have authority are subject to a higher standard and rightly so. Let us also remember that they are real humans with real fears and feelings. Hoping to return home to their families, they risk their lives daily to preserve the security we all so value. They sacrifice in ways unspoken and see things that would give us all nightmares. It's wrong to stereotype all black people; the same is true about all white people. Shouldn't the same apply to blue people? I know this message is not very popular right now, and I'm not sure if it will even be heard in this climate. He who has an ear, let him hear this word of caution; nothing good comes from a total disregard and disrespect of authority. What do you think will happen if all the good cops decide to quit (several have already) out of frustration because we have painted them with a broad brush, created an even more hostile environment against them, and have handcuffed them by limiting their ability to meet force with a necessary but responsible level of force? "If something strange go down in our neighborhood, who are we going to call?" It would have to be Ghostbusters because there will be no one else to call if police feel that they have an impossible job.

Again, this is not to insult the issue of police brutality, public lynching, racial profiling, wrongful imprisonment, and corruption. Wrong is wrong and requires systematic reform, but two or three wrongs (looting, killing, violence, and hating) doesn't make a right. It's dishonoring to the cause, and it validates police use of brutal force. I don't care how angry (be angry but sin not) we are, looting is injustice to the business owners, as well as to the community. The systematic killing of black people is injustice as well as the killing of police officers. We must call out that which is wrong but must also give honor where honor is due. Thank you to the men and women in blue; your souls matter too! The cry for justice is for all.

Injustice anywhere is a threat to justice everywhere. (Dr. Martin Luther King Jr.)

Offenses Leads to Hate

> And so I say to you on this occasion—*others
> may hate you, but those who hate you don't win
> unless you hate them.* And then you destroy your-
> self. (President Richard Nixon)

The power to hate or love in the midst of egregious offenses is determined by the condition of the hearts that filter them. In Luke 17 of the Holy Bible, Jesus warns us of offenses and how we should forgive them. Offenses are unavoidable. At some point, we will offend someone, and someone will offend us. As a matter of fact, this very message may be taken as offensive. In today's society, it seems as though everyone is offended; everyone feels as though they have been wronged. As the cries for justice get louder and louder, the message has become distorted; and we now live in a hypersensitive society that if we even look at someone too long or not look at them at all, they are offended; God forbid if we bump into them. The chip on most folks' shoulders is the size of Texas, and it does not take much to blow it off. I have observed a black and white person essentially make the same comment about a situation. The black person got a sign of agreement from all who were listening. The white person (who I might add has mixed race grandbabies whom he loves and is not ashamed of), got immediately accused of being a racist. He was told that there were certain things as a white man he should not say. The statement he said was true, but there was an automatic assumption made about the motives of the white man's heart to do harm. In this situation because of a spirit of offense (wounded hearts), whether or not the comment was true, it didn't even matter. The focus was on the messenger and not the heart of message. Why are people so offended these days? We are offended while driving, while on our jobs, while in church, and even by history which can't be changed or erased but only learned from.

In today's society, bias narratives are accepted as ones' truth, instead of the truth, and rebellion against authority is a medal of honor and glorified. No one wants to be corrected or told what to do

these days even if the correction is for their own protection. What will
be the harvest of the next generation as a result of these seeds being
planted? Lawlessness! Why have so many fallen in this trap of being
offended of everything? An offense is a trap set by Satan. He knows
that if He can get society in this trap that love will diminish, and hate
will take its place. In Matthew 24, Jesus talks about the last days;
and interesting enough, He talks about offensives and the dimin-
ishing of love in verse 10–12: "And then shall many be offended,
and shall betray one another, and shall hate one another. And many
false prophets shall rise, and shall deceive many. And because iniquity
shall abound, the love of many shall wax cold." Satan wants us to
literally "hate the hell out of each other" because if he can get us to
hate each other, in our hearts, we would not have enough room to
love God. It is impossible to hate others and love God, and this is the
trap that has been set for us all. Satan's ultimate goal is to get us to
be offended or to feel that we have been wronged by God. He wants
us to hate God. When things do not happen for us the way we want
them to, Satan comes to us to accuse God just as he goes to God to
accuse us to God; in the same manner, he accuses us to each other.
He is the father of divisiveness. Revelation 12:10 refers to him as the
accuser of the brethren. We should not allow ourselves to be so easily offended, but we should always walk in love because love covers
offensives or wrongs which is a mercy we all will someday need. It
keeps us in fellowship with God and with one another.

What Is Justice, and How Should We Achieve It?

A riot is the language of the unheard. (Dr.
Martin Luther King Jr.)

The things we sow, we shall reap. The scales of justice always
have two sides. If both sides are not weighed equally, it's called injustice. According to Proverb 11:1, "A false balance is abomination to
the LORD: but a just weight is his delight." Justice matters to God.
But righteousness also matters to Him which means we can be angry

about injustice, but we shouldn't sin in the process. According to Ephesians 4:26–27, "Be ye angry, and sin not: let not the sun go down upon your wrath: neither give place to the devil."

The world's view of justice can be summed up in this phrase "an eye for an eye," which means you hurt me, then I have a right to hurt you, and if you hate me, then I have a right to hate you. The hurt and the hate never ends with this ideology. What is different in God's view and the world's view? It is mercy; it is forgiveness. Because of sin, we all deserve death, instead God gave us mercy, and a way of escape through Jesus. He was our example. Now, death is still on the table because He is just, but we choose. The same is true about how we go about getting justice for ourselves. We choose every day in our hearts. We must die to ourselves so that others may go free. Now, why do I want them to go free? Well, they must go free in order for me to be free. *We choose to build walls or bridges every day with our hearts.*

Division comes when we take sides, but unity and understanding can be established if we take a look at both sides and give the same considerations. Seeing things one-sided will always keep us away from the truth because the scale has two sides. We should understand that the scale we use against others will be the same scale used against us. The judge of all, God, is watching our hearts and see if we tip the scale to one side or the other. If we show no mercy in our hearts, we shall receive no mercy; but if we show mercy in our hearts, we shall receive mercy and that from God. After all, that's justice! If by showing mercy changes a life for good, that's still justice!

> If it be possible, as much as lieth in you, live peaceably with all men. Dearly beloved, avenge not yourselves, but rather give place unto wrath: for it is written, Vengeance is mine; I will repay, saith the Lord. Therefore, if thine enemy hunger, feed him, if he thirst, give him drink; for in so doing thou shalt heap coals of fire on his head. Be not overcome of evil, but overcome evil with good. (Romans 12:18–21)

My son's name is justice; every so often, people ask me why I named him justice. In the season before his birth, our true enemy, Satan, stole from us. I called my son justice because every time I call his name, I want to be reminded of God's ability to right that which is wrong. We have to trust God for the justice we seek, for God can do far more than anyone on earth can do. Justice is fairness or to do that which is right. How do we know what's right? Who gave us the sense to understand what's right and what is wrong? We can't possibly know what's right if we have never experienced that which was wrong, and we couldn't possibly know what's wrong if we have never experienced that which is right. This sense of understanding what is just and unjust comes from God, so if justice comes from God, shouldn't we humbly appeal to Him when things doesn't seem quite right? One day soon, all of this shall be over. You and I will have to stand before a just and a Holy God.

God is not mock; what a man sows he shall reap. The price for sin (lust, hate, lying, murder, stealing, etc.) is death. That's God's justice, but I thank God that he is also merciful. His mercy is Jesus which is the only person that can pay the debt of death we all owe. We all love to shout justice as if it is only in our power to give or get, but God is ultimately the administrator of justice. Do not be blind to the fact that the justice we want from others will be the same sword that will come to us one day demanding justice. We all must understand that someday, we all will need mercy; and without it, all is lost. Satan is very clever in that he creates a situation of injustice and whispers to us long enough to be offended. Naturally, we become angry; and then more than likely, we will become unreasonable. Our lack of understanding causes bitterness, and from bitterness comes hatred. When our spirit gets contaminated with hatred, another spirit, demonic in nature, takes over. Until we repent and forgive, that which is right is wrong in our eyes, and that which is wrong is right in our eyes. We become victims of the lies of Satan. At this point, only truth and the love of Jesus can deliver us. Let man's process runs its course and, if need be, appeal to God. In the meantime, let's not destroy everything, each other, and even ourselves with the disease of hate.

> Returning hate for hate multiplies hate, adding deeper darkness to a night already devoid of stars. Darkness cannot drive out darkness; only light can do that. Hate cannot drive out hate, only love can do that. (Dr. Martin Luther King Jr.)

Always remember that in the end, God balances the scale. Man can only judge a thing by what they know, but God is a righteous judge who is all knowing. Though at times we may not understand why, just remember that God can see why. Whereas men fail, God always gets it right. Love never fails; and God's plan, even though we don't understand it at times, will never fail. So when it looks like we are losing, just know that everything we need to win has already been done for us on the cross. When we can't bear the situation or trial, Jesus will bear it for us; we must put all of our energy in just simply trusting Him. In time, our decision to do so will prove to be wise because He will never let you down.

But the Lord said unto Samuel, Look not on his countenance, or on the height of his stature; because I have refused him: for the Lord seeth not as man seeth; for man looketh on the outward appearance, but the Lord looketh on the heart. (1 Samuel 16:7)

It is the content of the heart that makes the man who he is whether that is good or evil. There is no racism in God, and if we belong to Him, His spirit should be in our hearts. His Spirit should override every evil thought toward others, especially those who do not look like us, that comes to mind.

Home Is Where the Heart Is

How we view life is shaped by the family we come from. The answer to all that is wrong or right in life begins with the family. Love, hate, and how we relate to the world outside our home are taught either by example or conversations. Let's talk about "the talk" that so many people affectionally mention that they have to have with their sons and daughters. Are our conversations with our children filled with love, wisdom, faith, understanding, and truth? Or are they filled with our fears, hate, bitterness, resentment and unforgiveness? A conversation is always important to have with all children, but the message they receive will determine if things truly change in the future. What goes on in the home will eventually show up on the streets of our communities. A student I taught many years ago wrote me about his experience in my class. He gave me permission to share this:

> Mr. Whitt, I'm one of your former students from Swartz upper elementary. You were my physical education teacher but you were also a mentor to me. I'm messaging you today because I wanted you to know that your lessons you taught me are still on my mind, especially during times like this. One of the most crucial lessons I learned occurred after I had gotten into a confrontation with another kid whom was black. I used the N word out of ignorance. I had no idea the meaning behind such a demeaning word. Not until you pulled me to the side and kindly taught me the lesson. This lesson was the foundation for one of the pillars I built my life upon. Understanding and equality. I want you to know that because of this lesson I refused to let my family's racism pass on through me. I began to confront my family on racism as well. You created a change, through me, that I will pass on to my children and my children will pass on to theirs. I hope you and yours are safe during this time. Good better best. Never let it rest. Until the good becomes the better, and the better becomes the best."

To God be the glory for this testimony because it was He who placed it in my heart to show my students, most of whom didn't look like me, the love of God. How we conduct ourselves will have generational implications. How we handle this moment will be the burden our children's children will bear. If we want change, it's starts with the heart, and this lesson starts at home. Our mission should always be to be the change we seek; if it's love, acceptance, and value we seek, we have to love, accept, and value others, including ourselves. This produces real change because everyone can recognize acts of kindness and love (God) in a person's heart. This love has the power to impact generations. This love is a choice and not an emotion; this love has no conditions attached to it. *You don't have to love me for me to love you. I choose to walk in love. You may not deserve my love, but love (God) paid for you to be deserving.* This love is a God-like love. It is something in each of us that we so desire this love and acceptance. Hate pushes people away, but Love, God's love, draws them in; it never fails. We are never more like our Heavenly Father than when we show mercy, forgiveness, and love! So, if we really want change, it must first start with our own hearts.

The Holy Bible asks a very challenging question, "What reward have you to only love those who love you?" To love someone that doesn't love you simply because of your status, class, race, ethnicity, etc., is a personal cross that most of us find difficult to bear. Even the civility of tolerance or being tolerated is no consolation for the pain of the subtle unjust rejection we feel. The undercurrent of hate and fear swirling in the atmosphere as a destructive tornado spreads when what's dormant deep in one's heart is resurrected to life by the breath of offense. We find ourselves guarding our hearts, not letting anyone in and not letting ourselves out. What is an offense but simply a game of "you hurt me so I must hurt you back" which leads to hating—a hate that in the long run perpetuates more hurt in one's life. *It's a natural thing to hate what hurts us, but it is a supernatural thing to love in spite of what or who hurts us.*

The issue of racism is simply ignorance of how to heal what hurts. For every action or belief, there is a cause. To find or to come face to face with what truly is behind the cause whether it be tradition, heritage, fear, lack of understanding, inferiority/superiority complex, or more than likely, just the influence of our true enemy, Satan, our hearts will be fooled into justifying the unmerciful acts of that which is the opposite of love. As a result of our fallen nature, this seed of hate is in each of us; whether it grows in us will be determined by the voices, experiences, and influences we allow to pour into us and to flow through us.

> But he that hateth his brother is in darkness, and walketh in darkness, and knoweth not whither he goeth, because that darkness hath blinded his eyes. (1 John 2:11)

Has Anything Changed? Time Is supposed to Change Us

> Our lives begin to end the day we become silent about things that matter. (Dr. Martin Luther King Jr.)

Have we turned into the direction we were growing from? Our history is a place from which we are supposed to grow. Are we still looking back and living in places that no longer exist? A place called the past. Has our memory caused us to relive the hurt and pain of injustice, rejection, and racism? Hearing or experiencing racial injustice to most people feels like someone has ripped the scab off of a festering wound, and the pain of that wound is relived afresh. This wound will never heal until the infection of hate is drawn out of it, and we allow the healing balm of love and authentic forgiveness (Jesus) to cover the wrong that's been done to us. Only then will the healing begin, and only then will we not continue to suffer from dead things we give life and power to. Most of our troubles come from our memories because memories not only preserve the time and experiences but also the pain of those experiences and of those times.

Are ye not then partial in yourselves, and
are become judges of evil thoughts? (James 2:4)

Whites Only

I remember going into a restaurant called the Burger Barn in this small town (Olla, Luisiana) on the way to my grandparent's house in Bayou Chicot (Ville Platte), Louisiana. My parents wanted to stop and get a couple of burgers. In 1983, I was about five years old; although I was so young, I remembered so vividly my dad and I standing in line as one white customer after another one was served while the cashier would not even acknowledge that we were standing there. My dad stood there quietly until he looked at me and told me, "Let's go." The look on his face then I didn't quite understand, nor did I understand why he didn't mention the incident to my mother. But he only said that we were going to get burgers somewhere else. Was it anger, shame, or hurt on his face that I saw that night? I did not understand what had just occurred at the time, but that was my first encounter with racial discrimination. It didn't feel good then, and today it still feels the same.

A History Lesson

I remember watching *Roots* by Alex Haley for the first time at the age of nine. I watched in disbelief of how people who looked like me were being treated by the people who didn't look like me. I saw chains, whips, beatings, rapes, tortures, kidnappings, killings, and the worst thing you can do to a people, which is to take away their freedom, identity, and dignity. Most of us have heard of the horrors of the past; but now, with a visible illustration of the atrocities and evil practices of slavery, it was as if we ourselves were personally experiencing the pain of what our people had endured. I remembered feeling so angry and confused. The day after *Roots* aired, most black folks, including myself, had a huge chip on our shoulders. I heard several of my black friends say, "I wish a white person would say something to me today." The tension that day was so thick in the air that it was almost visible, and everyone was on edge waiting for an explosion to occur. Thank God that there were only a few incidences but nothing major. The anger and the resentment from both sides was tangibly clear.

Roots told and showed us the truth of the atrocities suffered by African Americans at the hand of evil men. I believe even most white folks were shocked at what they saw. It showed us how wicked the heart of men can get due to his greed, thirst for control, and lust for power. Do I think airing shows like "Roots" or "Uncle Tom's Cabin" are a mistake? No! I think things that remind us of the past should give us an appreciation of just how far we have come. *We should forgive the past, be thankful for the presence, and do better in the future.* God saw the injustice and heard the cry of my people. He sent good men both black and white to put an end to such an evil practice which is a stain on the history of our country. *Love does not excuse the past, but love helps us to move on from the past.*

Real Estate's Unspoken Rule

I was about seven years old when my parents divorced; but it was in 1987 when my brother and I moved with my mother to a small neighborhood East of Monroe, Louisiana, called Love Estates. When we moved there, only four out of about two hundred families where black. I was also one of two black kids in my class at school, but that experience is another story. The people in my neighborhood seemed nice enough, but as the years went by, we started seeing more and more for-sale signs go up in the neighborhood. By the time I was a teenager, a quarter of the families in Love Estates were black families. That trend continued on until I moved out of Love Estates at the age of twenty. Today, Love Estates is about 98 percent black. What I witnessed but did not know at the time was what is called "white flight." Now whether or not it was racially motivated or economically motivated, only God and those individuals know their motives.

Culture Shock: From Being in the Office to Having an Office

> If you can't fly then run, if you can't run
> then walk, if you can't walk then crawl, but what-
> ever you do you have to keep moving forward.
> (Dr. Martin Luther King)

At the age of seven, I moved from a predominantly black school to a predominantly white school. I went from being surrounded by all black students to being the only male black student in my class. I had an inner struggle to fit in, but it seemed no matter what I did, I came up short. Everyone made sure I knew that I was black. I was just the black kid made to believe I was inferior. The N word was used against me frequently; and in retaliation, I would us the H word, which didn't change anything. As a result, being outnumbered, I eventually believed the inferior label given me and even the lies in my own head. The Bible says, "So as man thinks, so is he." My grades dropped dramatically, and I misbehaved because I didn't want to be invisible or ignored anymore. I didn't seem to care if the attention was for good or for bad. I didn't know who I was or what the future held for me. I was lost. Fear and hopelessness had their way with my mind, leading me to fail the fourth grade. I can remember when my mother took me over to my dad's house to tell him the news. He turned his back. I had never seen my dad so disappointed. My mother felt so sorry for him that she told him she held me back. In my heart, I never wanted to disappoint him again. I just didn't know how not to do that again. I just continued my downward spiral.

My last day as a student at this predominately white school ended with me getting into it with a white student, and I was facing a paddling or suspension. My teacher said that she was tired of me and sent only me to the office. I felt discriminated against, but the truth is that I was an angry child still recovering from the drastic changes in my life and my parents' divorce. I felt as though everyone and everything was against me. I was against myself.

My mom somehow knew I was struggling. She knew I needed help, so she enrolled me into the school where she worked. She simply wanted to have me close to her so she could keep a close eye on me. I hated leaving the predominant white school, and I can still remember looking back as we walked to my mom's little Datsun car. Little did I know that in the future, that would be one of three times I would leave this predominately white school.

At the age of nine, I had to face another drastic change which was a culture shock for me. It proved to be the best thing that could have happened to me. The school my mother worked at was a predominate black school in the city, and the facilities paled in comparison to the predominately white school. All of the children were African American except one white boy. To this day, I still wondered where he came from. I'm sure his experience must have been challenging just as mine was at the predominately white school. At this city school, the kids seemed harder and more knowledgeable about adult things. I felt so out of place even though we shared the same skin color. I, needless to say, wasn't a happy camper at first. On my first day, some of the boys were calling me names in front of the whole class. They would talk about my teeth or the clothes my mother made me wear. Almost every night, my mother and I would fight over what she wanted me to wear the next day. The second day of school, one of the boys asked to go to the restroom, and I asked shortly after he did. I had planned to teach him a lesson. I called his name down the hall. He looked. I asked him, "What was all that stuff you were talking about in class?" He started running toward me, so I did the only logical thing I could do—I ran! The spirit was willing, but the flesh was weak. I knew then that I wasn't in Kansas. My parents didn't raise a fool. I befriended one of the toughest guys at the predominately black school to make sure I wouldn't have any future problems. Terry, nicknamed Lil Hulk, and I became inseparable. He was tough, but he also was smart and wanted something out of life. Both he and I met a teacher that would forever change our lives.

Mr. Higgins's influence changed the course of my life. He had a very stern demeanor, and he looked like Malcolm X. He seemed very knowledgeable about life and about how we all fit in it. At the time,

I was still barely getting by with Ds, and I had a broken self-image and a warped mentality. He looked at me and basically said that there was more in me than I was revealing. In my mind, I was thinking, "Where?" He helped me create a vision. He told me that I could make the honor roll. He said that the sky was the limit and that I could be and do anything I wanted in life. He told me that I was not a failure. Looking back, I realize that this man was sent by God to reach me because I was lost. Finally, I took him at his word. He showed me the way, and I followed.

It was his caring that impacted me the most. He spent time with me, reassured me that I could do anything I set my mind to. He helped me set goals, and he believed in me. He helped me combat the negative forces in my head by giving me motivational books to read, books about people who were counted out but whose spirits would not die. These people overcame obstacles that erased any excuse I had not to succeed. They believed in these words "Greater is He that is in me than he that is in the world." They knew that no one has ever become a success on his or her own. These sayings and others reso-nated in my heart. Mr. Higgins taught me one saying that I lived by and now admonish others to live by. "Good, better, best never let it rest until the good becomes the better and the better becomes the best." Mr. Higgins helped me create a vision for myself which helped me see beyond my circumstances. The Bible says, "Where there is no vision, the people perish." That was exactly what was happening to me before God sent me help. I was drowning in self-pity, and I had a victim mentality. I believed the state I was in was everyone else's fault. I blamed myself, as well as my parents, God, the whites, and now even the blacks. I realized that I couldn't blame the whole world. Life was just happening to me. If we live long enough, life will happen to us. If the world unfairly knocks us down, with God's grace, we must pick ourselves up and dust ourselves off. I had to learn to forgive in order to move forward. Unforgiveness is like a weight that will hold a person in the past and forfeit his or her future. *Releasing others released me into my destiny.* My experiences at both schools prepared me for the diverse world we live in. I had learned to be all things to all people.

This story took about twenty-two years to develop, so to make a long story short. The people who saw me as trouble, instead of seeing a troubled kid, got the chance to see God's glory in my story. I went back to the predominately white school as a teacher for four years, and after leaving again and then moving back from Florida, I returned to this predominately white school and became the assistant principal. Of course, my journey didn't stop there because I left this predominant white school for the third and final time. If we don't learn the lesson from our pain, God has a way of re-enrolling us in the same class until we learn the lesson of love and forgiveness—lessons that bring glory to His name.

Secrets of the Heart

> In the end, we will remember not the words
> of our enemies, but the silence of our friends.
> (Dr. Martin Luther King Jr.)

In the year of 1989, I had one of the toughest experiences because I lost a friend or at least someone I thought was my friend. He and his family moved across the street from me with his sister, mom, and dad. His dad, who was Mexican, was the nicest guy you would ever meet; he was a plumber and occasionally, when my mom had plumbing trouble, he would help her free of charge. His wife, on the other hand, who was white, did not have much to say to me or my family. She worked a job in which she was gone a lot. I didn't notice then, but later, I realized that I was only invited to their house or was allowed to spend a night when she was not there. My friend's dad would make cinnamon rolls for us in the morning, and to this day, cinnamon rolls are my favorite desert. My friend and I had so much fun playing and trading cards every day.

I thought we would be friends forever, but all of that changed when one day, I was at my friend's house and his mom unexpectedly came home. He told me to hide in the front closet. She came in, and it did not take her long before she started making comments about the black kids walking down the street. She then said, "Those N word need to go home." And then there were shush and whispers followed by silence. The next word I heard came from her. She said, "Darnell, come on out." I came out, but I ran straight through the front door; needless to say, I never step foot in their door again. I don't know what she said to my "friend," but we were never friends again. He went from being a close friend to calling me the N word in which unfortunately, he paid for dearly. He started out like his dad but ended up like his mom. Later, his parents got a divorce, and they moved away. I heard several years later that his mom died at a young age. I pray that she was able to make things right with God before she transitioned. I also ran into his dad several years later, and he was still just as nice as he was many years ago.

The Forbidden Fruit

In 1994, it was still taboo in Monroe, Louisiana, for a black boy to date a white girl; so when an unlikely high-profile love affair developed between me and a white cheerleader, we were the talk of the school. Some people were supportive, but a lot of white guys did not like it. They had written her off as trash or a loose girl, to put nicely. There was also another group that didn't like it, and that was black girls. Many of them didn't like me because of it. Well eventually, word had gotten back to the white young ladies' older brother, and he in turn sent word that I better leave his sister alone. Before long, I received a phone call from her crying. She said that she was sorry, but she could not see me anymore. I could tell that someone was listening to her tell me of our break-up because she certainly wasn't herself. I would like to believe that it was more than just a curiosity between us, but at that age, who knows. After that, when no one was looking, she would give me a look, and I knew exactly what her eyes were saying. We both shared a difficult experience with each other which, to a certain extent, has created a chapter in our lives we shall never forget, and to this day, although still traveling down different roads, we are still friends.

The Issues of Race, Racism, and Elitism

We have to deal (diagnose and address) with the issues of race, racism, and elitism with raw truth and transparency. Until we are willing to admit our faults, we are bound to repeat our transgressions to God, as well to each other. If we do not deal with the issues, we will continue to live with the issues. In order for hearts to heal, with and to each other, we must be real, even if it hurts. Truth has to hurt before it can heal.

There is one race with different shades of color. We all came from one man and one woman to form the one race called the human race. "And hath made of one blood all nations of men for to dwell on all the face of the earth, and hath determined the times before appointed, and the bounds of their habitation" (Acts 17:26) The bottom line is that racism or a belief that one's own race is superior and has the right to dominate other races seen as inferior based on differences is a sin. "But if ye have respect to persons, ye commit sin, and are convinced of the law as transgressors" (James 2:9). At some point in our lives, if we are honest, we have all been guilty of this at some level. Whether it be blatantly obvious or subtle in thought, we who are in Christ should not act upon those thoughts but cast them away in the name of Jesus. The easiest way to avoid the sin or the trap of racism is to walk in truth (be honest with yourself and others) and unconditional love (the love that only God in us can produce). Without the love of God, coming face to face with a racist draws every ounce of hidden racism or elitism within us to manifest, and then the fight begins. Love sees a racist or an elitist as a victim of Satan; and it is the same love that can destroy the issues of race, racism, or elitism in our own hearts.

There is a root of racism in America, and the ground from which it grows is in our hearts. Subtle, most times it may be, but it is found in the attitudes and preferences we embody which is passed down from generation to generation. The enemy knows that division causes weakness. It's called divide and conquer, and for too long, we have all been victims of this tactic. We have been baited to fight or war against each other for one purpose and one purpose only, our destruction in the end.

Two Wrongs Never Makes It Right

Let no man pull you so low as to hate him.
(Dr. Martin Luther King Jr.)

On October 3, 1995, I heard a roaring cheer in the hallways of my high school from black students about the acquittal of OJ Simpson who was accused in the double murder of his white wife and her white "boyfriend." I truly believed that everyone believed that he was guilty, but as stated by a former Simpson juror, Carrie Bess, this was payback for the beating of Rodney King and subsequent acquittal by the officers involved a couple of years earlier. Most of my white classmates were shocked and angry because a black man had gotten away with murder. My black friends argued that white people had been getting away with murder since the beginning of time. Black students did not hide how they felt about it as they chanted OJ's lawyer Johnnie Cochran Jr.'s famous coined phrase, "If it don't fit, you must acquit." That day, most black people felt vindicated from all of the injustices they could think of that had been done to them. It was something they could rub in the faces of their white "oppressors." In all of this, it did not seem to matter that a man was, without mercy, almost beaten to death; it did not seem to matter that two people's lives were cut short. This alone showed us just how imperfect man's justice can be. It also shows the condition of our hearts, hearts that need Jesus.

My Skin Is My Sin

I never had to worry about a ride to work, church, or school; I always had a white friend to do that for me. During that time, the only friends of mine in high school who had cars, given to them by their parents, were white with a few exceptions. The summer of

1996, at the age of eighteen, I finally saved enough money to purchase my first car which was an El Dorado Cadillac. My brother and I decided to go for a ride one day. Shortly after driving through a predominantly white neighborhood, a policeman pulled us over. I knew that I was not speeding because we were just cruising.

When the white officer made it to my widow, I said, "Hello, officer, what exactly did I do?"

He said, "Let me see your license, registration, and proof of insurance."

I said, "Okay."

He took my information and walked back to his car. By this time, my brother and I was trying to figure out what I did wrong, but we simply could not come up with anything. When the officer returned, I asked him, again, "What did I do wrong?" And He politely said that we looked suspicious being two young black men driving a car like this (rims) and riding through a white neighborhood (Granted, I lived right down the road). My brother was furious and was about to say something; I looked at him as to say, "Shut your mouth!"

I turned to the officer and said, "Thank you, sir!" I understood that he was the authority, and he was just doing his job. We drove off with no incident except with the knowledge of knowing what it felt like to be racially profiled.

Even in Death

At the end of my junior year in high school, a dear friend of mine, who happened to be a white female, tragically died in a car accident. Just days before, I saw her for the last time as she smiled and walked away. She loved reading my poetry. Before she walked away, she told me that she wanted to read my latest writings. As you already know, that never happened. In fact, the next poem I wrote was about her life. Someone shared it with her family, and they wanted me to read it at her funeral. They were so broken, and this poem gave them something to make sense of their loss. A couple of days after the funeral, I went to their house to check on them.

They hugged my neck and cried. I could tell that her father had been drinking probably to numb the pain. As I talked with her father, he told me that a couple of his friends, in the midst of his grief, asked him what was a black boy doing writing poems about his daughter. He told me that he told them to shut up and stay away from him. As tears fell from his eyes, he said that I was always welcome at his house. He told me to pray for him and to stay in touch. Love has a way of breaking barriers and changing lives for Christ.

Home Away from Home

It was 1997, right before my senior year in high school. I had decided to go workout at the school that day for summer workouts. Two white guys came up to me and just started talking as if we had known each other for years. They were brothers and had just moved here from out of state (I think New Mexico). After workouts, they invited me to their home to play pool. I decided to go, and that is when I met their parents. Apparently, the apple didn't fall too far from the tree because they were just as friendly and talkative. The boy's mom was extremely attentive, and she had a way of making you feel as though you were the most interesting and important person in her world. To make a long and interesting story short, that same year, I went through a very trying time in my life. This family became my family, and they treated me as if I was one of their own. I learned so much about life from them, and I lived on and off with them for three years while I finished college. I am forever grateful for this experience because this is why I give everyone the benefit of the doubt. Color isn't the first thing I notice about a person; it is what they say because it gives me a clue of what's in their heart. Just as this family, I am more interested in who you are as a person than I am interested in what shade of color your skin was blessed with.

In between 1997–2006, I had so many black, white, Hispanic, and even mixed-race people help me along the way. Life is a journey that is very difficult to make it alone. I owe my success to a diverse group of people God has placed in my path.

My Wealth in Friends

In 2006, I visited a couple of friends from church in Pensacola, Florida. I had expressed my desire to them about moving there, but I needed to find a job in the school system. A mutual friend, who was white, heard our conversation. He picked up the phone and called a friend, and just like that, I had an interview the next day. I had a short interview with a nice black duty superintendent of Escambia county schools, and before I knew it, I had the job. The timing was perfect. I knew that I was right in the middle of the will of God. I moved to Pensacola, Florida, for an opportunity to gain the experience I was told I needed in order to get a job as a school administrator in Ouachita Parish. At the time, I was only twenty-seven years old and thought maybe I would just stay in Florida. All of that changed when my former white coach and superintendent of Ouachita Parish schools called me with an opportunity in Monroe, Louisiana. The only thing I had to do was to teach the remaining three months at a middle school, and he promised to help me achieve my goal the following year. I was a little homesick, and I could not turn down this opportunity. He would later stay true to his word and hire me as one of the youngest ever black assistant principals in Ouachita Parish. Yet before this could happen, I had only a couple of weeks to report to the job, but I didn't have a place to live. In telling a friend, who was white and married to a Hispanic woman, that I was moving back home, he asked me where I was going to live. I told him that I was in the process of looking; he immediately offered his upstairs bedroom to me for as long as I needed it. Now that I had a place to stay, I had to figure out how I was going to move with such short of a notice. I donated most of my furniture to the church that I was attending in Florida, and they gave me a small check to help with my moving expenses. I still had more stuff than my car could hold. Out of the blue, an old white friend of mine from college called me. I told him that I was in the process of moving back, and I also told him about my situation. He immediately said that he would come help me with his trailer once he got off from work the following day. He got off from work and drove six and a half hours straight to Pensacola; and within a few hours after he took a nap, we loaded up and drove back to Monroe, Louisiana. Regardless of his color, how many people do you know would volunteer for something like that? I'm sure very few people. My success in life is not my own, but it first belongs to God and then friends like this who happen to come from all walks of life.

Bridge Builder

According to a prophetic word I received years ago, God has called me to be a bridge between the races, and I have seen evidence of that through the many experiences I have had in my life, experiences where I have seen the good, the bad, and the ugly. I grew up as a black Baptist, but then God called me to serve in several different interracial and denominational churches over the years. He was teaching me about people, and boy, did I learn. The church that I am currently serving at, many years ago, used to be a church with the reputation of turning away black people. This heritage and practice was anti-God, and it was not a reflection of God but a reflection of the hearts of men whom, in time, God has changed (with their permission, of course). My presence now at this church shows me and others the conditions of our hearts as we interact with each other. As I followed the calling of the Lord, I was asked to serve on the church board. I have served on the board for over fourteen years with the respect of my white brothers on that board. They valued my opinion and considered my ideas and concerns. God is always up to something; we can't allow ourselves to be so hurt by people that we limit God on how he can use us.

> Let nothing be done through strife or vainglory; but in lowliness of mind let each esteem other better than themselves. Look not every man on his own things, but every man also on the things of others. (Philippians 2:3–4, KJV)

When I Needed It Most

About seven years later after moving back from Pensacola and only being married for a year, my mother-in-law was killed, on her way to meet her newborn granddaughter named Hope in the hospital, by drug dealers running from the police in a high-speed chase. My wife and I were lying in bed when her phone rang about 11:30 p.m. We heard loud crying on the other end of the phone. My wife kept asking, "What's wrong?" They told her to give the phone to me. They explained to me what happened to my wife's mother and left me with the task of telling her. My wife was broken and in a state of shock. I called my pastor, who was white, to ask him to pray for us. At 12:30 a.m. in the morning, he came to our house to comfort my wife and support me. He told me that I needed to get my wife to her family as soon as possible. They lived one thousand miles away in Baltimore, Maryland. My pastor (PSW) told his associate pastor to get us first-class airplane tickets to Baltimore for the next morning. While we were there, for about two weeks, he continued to check on us. This man was white. Yet he did something he didn't have to do, and that was to care.

If we are not careful, our bad experiences will shape how we engage in relationships with others; and if our bad experiences outweigh our good experiences in our eyes, the taste that will be left in our mouths will be bitter. There is no end to the wickedness in man's heart once we begin to lose sight of the value and the meaning of every life. Once we lose the sanctity of every life, we lose our soul; and in the process, we lose sight of God. We should never only let our experiences with others determine how we see others collectively, but we should always see others through the eyes of Jesus, which is love. It will filter through all of the hurt and pain that stands in our way toward forgiveness and reconciliation. It will bring the healing we all so desperately need.

Along the way, I have experienced good and bad in different races. *There is a bad apple in every bunch, but I have learned that you can work around those bad apples and enjoy the fruit of all the good ones.* Finally, I've concluded that we are all different, yet we are all the same. We are just human beings experiencing life differently yet the same in some ways. We have come a long way, but many of us still believe that we have not come far enough. *Sometimes, the problems that present themselves in the present are the same old problems unresolved from the past. Time is supposed to change us and that for the better.* The past no longer exists in this present moment, but it is kept alive in us as long as we live there. Haunted by the shadow of bad experiences in life, our memories are as scars—visible reminders of the pain of the past. Experiences we carry with us throughout time can poison our hearts toward people we have not taken the time to get to know.

The sins of slavery and that of a nation was paid for by its sons and daughters during the Civil War. The judgement touched every home until the debt was paid in full. There is a price that must be paid for innocent shed blood, and that price requires blood, either the blood of Jesus or our own. *As we as African Americans are free today of the bondage of slavery, so are our white brothers and sisters free today from the bondage of slavery.* It is impossible to enslave others and not be a slave (to sin) yourself. *The end result of the Civil War (preceded by a National Day of Prayer) is what held our country together from secession; and again this same fight in our hearts and minds, if not won, will tear this country apart.*

> We must learn to live together as brothers or perish together as fools. (Dr. Martin Luther King Jr.)

In the echoes of our minds, if we are going to remember the past, remember it all which includes the good and the bad. If we are honest, our experiences in life should balance each other. We should, at some point, experience good where we expected nothing but bad and vice versa. Rudeness, discrimination, hate, racism knows no color because these are conditions of the heart; and last I checked, the color of everyone's heart is the same, which means these conditions can be found in us all.

The very definition of *prejudice* is a belief without adequate information (bases) or to put it plainly, ignorance. It is pure ignorance to stereotype a group of people based on some experiences we have had with them. Not everyone is the same, and thank God we are all different. *Our differences are supposed to be a blessing and not our curse.* Imagine a world in which everything such as color, taste, smell, or sounds were the same. God gave us diversity to experience the full beauty and the genius in His creation. We all are a part of something much bigger, and apart we take away from God's masterpiece. We all bring our unique qualities, abilities, and characteristics to the human experience. In each other, we have everything we need to display some of the glory in heaven on earth. I'm thankful for all of my experiences because they helped me to understand life from different perspective; and I've learned we all have the same fears, desires, and issues. We also have the same enemy, and it is not each other.

We all share a common enemy, and until we understand who he is, we will continue to hate each other. If we don't gain an understanding of the weapons Satan uses against us, we will continue to assassinate each other in our hearts and not really know why. The root of our problem is not with each other, but it is with the deceiver. Of course, influenced by him, we have done things to each other, but the Bible says be angry but sin not. If we don't deal with the root issue of the problem (starting with our own hearts), we will discuss every issue except the issue that will solve the problem. We will rehearse the pain of our wounds, instead of allowing them to heal. There is a deeper issue here, and it is not just black and white. Choosing sides closes the door to any possible solution; we have to choose to understand both sides and infuse love in every conversation. We have to be honest with ourselves and each other, seek truth, walk in peace, and be a bridge between both sides of the divide. We have to pray for each other, and we have to choose on purpose to reach out to those who do not look like us or think like us. We also have to make efforts toward those who don't like us. The only side we should be on is on the side of righteousness.

What Really Is the Matter, and What Should Matter

As a black man, I am nobody's victim. If there is a barrier to my success, I will go around it, descend under it, rise above it, or I will just burst through it. "Greater is He that is in me than he that is in this world." If a door closes, I will try another one; and if there is no door, well, in full confidence, I will just make one and walk right on in. Yes, my journey and my struggle may be harder than most; but guess what, if I faint not, I will be stronger than most. We have been physically emancipated only to be enslaved by invisible chains—untrained, uneducated, and set free only to bare chains of the mind that guarantees our poverty, lives stolen once before and now once again. Some fortunate souls have unlocked the chains through association; nevertheless, their scars are still there. God can't get glory out of a victim's story. No man writes my story, only God and the ability he has given me to be the author of my future. As I give you respect. I expect it in return. You can keep your welfare, your government assistance, and your Section 8 housing. I'm no longer anybody's slave. Don't give me anything, but if in your own pride, you just have to give me something to feel that I need you (indeed we need each other), just give me equal opportunity. (A Free Man)

When someone discovers our value, to the world we seem more valuable. We have been discovered, and we are on our way to stardom. In reality, our value has always existed even when no one recognized it. In the world, the value people place on us gives us value; but with God, value was already built in us. Whether we get discovered or not, our value never changes. Until our mind-set changes, nothing in our life will change. Our thoughts are the seeds of our actions, and how we conduct ourselves is how people will begin to see us if they are honest. If we have to tell someone that our lives matter, that must mean that we are still convincing ourselves. A millionaire does not go around saying that he is a millionaire; he knows it and doesn't care whether or not you know it or not. He is so confident in who he is that most time, he does not even dress like we think a millionaire should dress. No, it is those who are in debt who are flashy with their lifestyles. They scream, "Look at me. I am somebody." If we know who we are, we don't have to tell anybody because they will know. Our self-concept matters more than someone else's evaluation of our value.

> Free at last, Free at last, Thank God almighty
> we are free at last. (Dr. Martin Luther King Jr.)

There is never a question of whether or not anyone's life matters. God assigns value to life, but when people put themselves in the place of God, they feel as though they can determine the value of someone else's life. No one can make another person feel inferior unless they already see themselves as inferior, which is in direct opposition to what God created them to be which is free. Freedom is worth the fight no matter the cost. A man is born free. He should live free, and he should die free. Freedom is an inalienable right given from the Father above. To wrongfully violate one's freedom is as grievous as stealing one's soul. Freedom is the only way a man can truly live. Without it, he is already dead. The Son of God freed us, and who he frees is free indeed. He so valued us that he gave His life for ours. This alone should free us from the opinions of man because the only opinion that should really matter is the one who demonstrated our value through his sacrifice. We all matter to Christ, so boldly should we walk in that knowledge and not in the fear of any man. It's not who we are that holds us back. It is not knowing whose we are and what we are capable of that does. Knowing who we are and not what people say we are (slave name) should give us the confidence we need to tap into all of the potential inside of ourselves and do the things others wouldn't expect of us. It matters not what others say or do; it only matters what we say about and do for us. Not that it should matter, but this alone will show people who we are.

Evil has no face, no color, no age, no ethnicity, no class, no address, no preference, no occupation, no gender, no body type, no religion, and no political party. It is the spirit of the fear inspired by the devil himself. It is fear that causes us not to love—fear of rejection, fear of injustice, fear of being hurt, fear of being betrayed, fear of being called a racist, fear of not being counted, fear of the past, fear of being disenfranchised, fear of owning our own failures, fear of what we don't understand, and fear as a result of not feeling safe, all are barriers to loving others. Most of us focus on race or politics, but we all need to understand that the fight is not confined to our little categories. The fight is between the devil and God over us. The war has been won, so why are we still fighting? If we are going to fight, we must fight on the side of righteousness; we must let people know that we are Christ followers by the love we have for one another regardless of whatever differences we may have. The victory is in the spirit, but in the flesh, there is defeat. In the flesh, there is division. In the flesh, there is confusion. In the flesh, there is deception. In the flesh, there is death. By walking in the spirit, we walk in revelation, understanding, love, freedom, blessings, victory, and the light. We must be righteous in our living by living to love.

> He hath shewed thee, O man, what is good;
> and what doth the Lord require of thee, but to
> do justly, and to love mercy, and to walk humbly
> with thy God? (Micah 6:8)

The Bible tells us to train up a child in the way he should go, which suggest that there is a way he shouldn't go. Each family unit is responsible for training productive God-fearing citizens, citizens that value life (whether it's the unborn, the elderly, Asians, Hispanics, whites, and blacks etc.), citizens that have respect for themselves, the law, and authority, whether it's the authority of a parent, another adult, an elder, a teacher, a principal, a pastor, a law enforcement officer, and God (respect that is characterized as a level of fear or reverence for a person's position in another person's life, respect that produces humility in how one interacts with the symbols of authority in one's life).

Citizens that are confident in their ability and in their future: They do not lean on the crutch of victimization, but they take personal responsibility in their success regardless of the barriers, for they know how to climb. They know how to dig, and they are smart enough to navigate around the obstacles set up to impede their progress. In their eyes, there is no glass ceiling over their heads that they cannot shatter, and the sky is not the limit for them. They do not play the blame game or point fingers because they know that "greater is He that is in them than he that is in the world," and the only person that can stop them is themselves. They do not guilt people into accepting them because they know who they are, and they are accepted based on their own character, behavior, and merits. They know that if a person has a problem with their skin that that person doesn't have a problem with them but with God; and because of their character, they know to pray for that person.

Citizens that have a genuine love for all people regardless of their differences: They understand that there is more to a man than just the flesh that covers his bones, for every man has an eternal soul. They don't fear that which is different from them because they look at everyone through the lens of mercy and the filter of love. They don't look so much at a person's race or social status, but they look for decency in a person.

Citizens that give honor where honor is due: They know how to honor their parents, their leaders, and their God.

Citizens that give more than they take and the sacrifices of those before them: They know how to appreciate. They serve wherever there is a need, and they don't feel entitled to anything but a chance to love and be loved by everyone. They don't chase handouts, but they diligently seek those they can help up. They are a blessing to all who come in contact with them and not a burden. They understand that to whom much is given much is required. If they somehow found themselves in a position where they have little, they would still give their last because they know that it is more blesseth to give than to receive. They are thankful to God and have committed themselves to His work.

Citizens that will build rather than tear down: They repair the bridge instead of destroying it. They are tempered and possess self-control. They always look out for the best interest of others rather than being self-centered. They seek to become the solution and not a contributor to the problem. They are a voice of reason in the midst of confusion. They use their voice for good and never allow the platforms of fools to influence them. They are fully submitted to God and not the opinions of man.

Citizens that practice mercy and that are quick to forgive: They understand how much God have forgiven them. They understand that it easier to let people go rather than carrying them in the prison of their hearts. They know that God sees their heart, and how they respond (forgive) to others is how He will respond (forgive) to them.

Citizens that fight for what they believe in and are willing to die for a worthy cause: They are guided by their conscience and have learned how to quiet themselves so that they can hear the Holy Spirit (God). They understand that their own righteous is as filthy rages; they understand the condition of their own hearts and their need for God. They understand that the only way that they can be and live righteously is through Christ.

The issue we have in this world can be found in the training or lack of training of the children we have been entrusted with by God. An untrained child is everybody's problem. What goes on in the home will eventually show up on the streets of our communities. We, collectively, can't blame a person, a system, a race, our history, nor can we blame God. God gave us His plan for the family; He gave us His Word. We, collectively, had the responsibility to create the world we want to live in, yet so many of us have failed. Now is not the time to blame anyone, but it is time to get it right in our own homes. In the spirit of personal responsibility, this is the mindset we all need to embrace: change begins in me.

The time is always right to do what is right.
(Dr. Martin Luther King Jr.)

There is even a time for justice, and in due time, justice will come; until then, we are blessed if we desire peace, forgiveness, and reconciliation. In this season of justice, we must find a way to reconnect in order to produce real change. Change is our heart's cry, but how can things change if the hearts of men on both sides refuse to change? To refuse love is to invite hate. Many doubt whether or not we have made any progress at all. If you were to ask me if anything has changed, I would say yes. I would say that I have changed, as well as my experiences. Sometimes, when your situation does not seem to be changing, you have to ask God to change you for the situation. Progress and change begin with individuals and their own hearts. Now, I understand that this is a heart issue and not a skin issue. If I so happen to have another bad experience, I know how to counter it with unconditional love, and never again will I blame an entire race of people for the actions of a few foolish people. In order to have that wonderful life, I will not overlook all of my good experiences to only focus on the bad ones. *I shall never forget that love is a debt we all owe to each other.*

But I say unto you which hear, Love your enemies, do good to them which hate you, Bless them that curse you, and pray for them which despitefully use you. (Luke 6:27–28)

Father, forgive us for we know not what we do!

Selah 5:1–44

1. Respectfully and with all humility, this is a different perspective on a very sensitive issue. When we get to the point, we can't see things from a different viewpoint. Truth hides itself from our sight, and as the blind, we can only see through what we feel. *Both memorials of honorable and*

dishonorable men serve as a reminder of where we've been and a marker of how far we have come. To remove those memorials is to erase the story of the struggle for America's soul, the very struggle that contributed to our greatest triumphs and greatest failures. It is a reminder that though she is great, she is not perfect. Many atrocities have occurred on her soil, and from her wound, things have been birth that we still feel the effects of today. What she was and what she is now will determine what she will be in the future. To erase what she was gives future generations no reference of what she shouldn't become again. *History forgotten is a lesson lost.* Who will defy time and live to tell the story of Her (America) triumphs and tragedies? Whose shoulders will future generations stand on to see how much further we need to go? These statues are more than the simplistic symbols of heroes or symbols of hate we have made them; they are the unspoken truth of our becoming. The many stories behind them explains how we are, where we are, and why we are where we are. The coming together or formation of this nation involved all of our ancestors good or bad. The skills, the talents, the wit, the courage, the traditions, the heritage, the ethnicity, the cultures, and the faith all combined to make a unique and diverse place.

Now, all of this coming together didn't come without revealing the depravity of the heart of man, his greed, his lust, his prejudices, and his struggles. Some suffered more than others, but without our ancestors and their struggles, we wouldn't possess the strength we have today. It's up to us to tap into that collective strength and become all that they couldn't be. The sum total of everything that has happened (the good, the bad, and the ugly) has brought us all to this point. Everything is worth remembering, for when we lose our memory, the foundation of who we are ceases to exist. Our foundation (our history), whether we like or not, is the very thing that holds us up and keeps us together. It is the one thing, besides our creator (God-Yahweh) we all share. Our struggle, our journey, and our resilience has made us who we are. It's what we stand on, and it is what we can build on. We can handle the ugly truth. It's okay to remember the things that may hurt, for if we erase those things, we will never truly know if we have reached our point of healing. *Seeing the perceived symbols of hate and being around others whose stories is not exactly like ours uncovers the true condition of our hearts.* Facing those things that hurt is like looking into a mirror that will never lie to us. It's either ugly or it's pretty. *As any good therapist would tell you, in order to forgive, we have to remember and face the things we want to forget;* in other words, we have to take the scab off and deal with the infection before it spreads and before it's too late. It is only through our memories that we can truly be honest with how we truly feel and see the things, often suppressed or hidden, we need to forgive.

Justice can't bring healing because after another incident, in anger, we will have to seek it again. It's never satisfied (in the natural). The only way to truly heal is to forgive (something supernatural). True healing can take place if we would, instead of tearing memorials down, walk up to a dishonorable memorial and say, "I forgive you" (what a movement!). By doing so, we not only release them, but we release ourselves from the chains of hurt and the shackles of hate. We should leave them there for future generations to remember so that they may also have the opportunity to forgive that which so deeply divides us. There is another memorial I would like to mention; it's called a living memorial. Instead of tearing each other down, we should walk up to a dishonorable memorial and say, "I forgive you." Now if that doesn't prick the conscience of a person, nothing will; for in those words, if truly meant, are mercy and God. Always remember that our history together makes us who we are as Americans and as human beings—imperfect. That's worth remembering! What happened in the past should never be dismissed. There is always a reason for everything, and in those reasons is where the lessons can be learned. *Learning the lessons that make up the past is essential to any change in the future.* It is because we can stand on the shoulders of past that we can see and have direction for the future. Otherwise, we travel down the same old roads and make the same old mistakes later. Wisdom comes from having value in the experiences of those who have been there. The cost is free, and the benefits consist of understanding and a solid platform to build on. Life is one lesson after another, and those lessons support and build upon each other. To dismiss the past is as building on shifting sand.

2. This is a warning, especially to Christians, about guarding our hearts. This is meant to help and not to inflame the situation concerning the killing of an unarmed black man. It's okay to be angry, outraged, or even hurt because that is naturally understandable; but supernaturally, never lose sight of who the real enemy is. When we start giving evil a face or a color, we begin to hate people we don't even know. That is a very dangerous place to be in naturally or spiritually.

    Evil has no race, class, social status, or look. It's in my neighborhood, as well as your neighborhood, and it is even within each of us to do evil if not for the restraint of the love of God and the Holy Spirit. Evil can come in the form of physical murder or heart murder (hate). *"Everyone who hates his brother is a murderer, and you know that no murderer has eternal life abiding in him"* (1 John 3:15). Either form is not pleasing to God. *"If anyone says, 'I love God,' and hates his brother, he is a liar; for he who does not love his brother whom he has seen cannot love God whom he has not seen"* (1 John 4:20). What divides us will be the very thing that destroys us, if we let it. In witnessing unjust acts that personally impact us, such as the hunting of an innocent young man by two misguided individuals, we must guard our hearts. This was done by two people and not a whole race of people. Offenses are traps designed by Satan for our destruction. *Yes, seek justice but do not lose the heart of God in the process which is love for people who may not desire it.* We surely didn't deserve it. Love never fails, and in the end, Justice will prevail. *"Seek justice love mercy and walk humbly with your God"* Micah 6:8. Either we believe and abide by God's word or we let flesh have its way onto our own and those we bring with us destruction. Hatred is very contagious, and the masks we hide behind is not enough to stop it. It requires the heart and the blood of Jesus to deal with egregious atrocities such as the shedding of innocence blood. Trust me, Jesus knows how to deal with that. We must guard our hearts, be angry, but sin not.

3. We are the United States and not the Divided States. What divide us, if we let it, will destroy us. This nation was founded upon "one nation under God." That should be the common thread that brings us together, but sadly the tragedy that will finally bring us together will mean that it is almost already too late. Together we can stand, but divided we are vulnerable and subject to fall. Division is a weakness, but unity is our strength. In spite of our differences, we are Americans.

4. We all walk through the world differently yet somehow the same; how does the world see us? Is it through the wrinkles on our faces or the graying of our hair? Is it through the location of our home or the job title we hold? Is it through the church or the organizations we attend? Is through our ethnicity or the color of our skin? We all walk through the world differently because we are seen differently. This is the same reason that some of us walk through this world the same because we are seen as being the same. We are stereotyped regardless of our individual experiences in life. This is good for some but can be very bad for others. Is this right, or is this wrong? Is this just the way it is? We are all guilty! I'm reminded of an old saying that still rings true and teaches today: "Never judge a book by its cover." Yet some will say that the cover of the book, most times, is

an indicator of what the story will be about. My response: true, but what if we are wrong? How does prejudgment feel to us? How does having someone sum us up even before getting to know us feel? From my experience, it feels horrible. Dr. King said it best in his speech about judging a person by the content of their character. This requires getting to know a person beyond the casual hellos and "how do you dos." We all should remember that the character of the book is what makes the story. We must read the book first (spend quality time) before we come to any conclusions because things or people are not always what they appear to be good or bad. As we come to know the characters in the story, we will begin to realize that we are not so different that we can't relate (things that make us the same) to one another. We are humans. We are family.

5. Race is about position in a competition and isn't just the practice of. Racism is the practice of positioning oneself in a competition. It is about power, control, and domination over another group of people.

6. Now, racial prejudice is characteristic of relating to a belief about a group of people without adequate basis. It is ignorance in knowing that we are different, but not understanding or acknowledging the fact that we are all the same. We all came from the same two beings; we are one, the human race.

7. How we dress will give others information on how to address us. If we want to be liked, we must first like ourselves. If we want to be respected, we must first respect ourselves. If we want to be love, we must first love ourselves; we teach people how to treat us.

8. To feel important is what we all so desire. Why? Because there is something in us that tells us that we are, but over the years, the actions of others communicate that we are not. They communicate that we are not acceptable, and the pain of rejection erodes our security in who we are. We are supposed to be who God says we are, but as the scripture goes, "So a man thinks so is he." We were all uniquely

made; we all have the creator's signature on us. We are His masterpiece, a vital piece of the puzzle of life. No two people have the same fingerprints which means no two people will have the same impact on this world. We all have a special assignment from the one who gave us life; and that, my friend, is something special. Once we understand the value in people, we begin to see them differently. When we see them differently, hopefully they will begin to see themselves differently (as something of worth or value). We all matter to God, and because of this, we should matter to each other.

9. We are all born perfect for our purpose; how we got here is not as important as being here on a divine assignment to complete our life's task for the fulfillment of God's plan. Every life matters to God, and if we would see people through this lens, we would see them differently. Each individual's purpose is connected to each other to fulfill the perfect plan of God for humanity. This is why we need not see each other as a color or class, but we should see each other as brothers or sisters. We were designed for relationship because together, under the lordship of God, there is nothing on earth we can't accomplish. As we live, we write the chapters of our life stories. Before the foundations of the earth, we were known. This should give our lives a whole new meaning. The destiny that each individual carry is unknown to the one who carries it and others. In its appointed time, the destiny shall be revealed and released for all to marvel at. None of us have any idea of the potential that lays dormant in the people we interact with daily. If we knew and, for that matter, if they knew, how we engage with one another would change. We would then understand that none of us was created average, but we all are equipped with gifts that need to be developed. We all will only reach the potential we discover and develop.

10. People can be control with little fight by keeping them ignorant. This is why knowledge and information are essential to living a life of peace and freedom. As long as

there is breath in our bodies, we should be reading and learning something new. The legacy of slavery is illiteracy which leads to poverty; and from poverty, economically and/or spiritually, comes all the other issues. Our people are destroyed because of lack of knowledge.

11. We can become so used to or conditioned to someone feeding us to the point we refuse to lift a finger to feed ourselves. There has never been an enemy to us than the enemy we have been to ourselves. No one can do to us what we have done to ourselves. No one is the blame until we first acknowledge that we are to blame for so neglecting the power and potential within us; it is to ourselves we have not been true. There is no betrayal like the betrayal we can inflict upon ourselves. There is no lie like the ones we tell ourselves. There is no rejection like that of us rejecting ourselves but unable to separate from that which we reject. There is no injustice like the injustices of self-harm and self-hate, for they go against our inherent response of self-preservation. There is no evil like the evil found in a man's heart and his thoughts, for from his heart and his thoughts come all of the evil brought upon himself and others. There is no one that can pull and keep us down better than we can do to ourselves. There is no oppression like the oppression, governed by our own belief system, we allow to dictate our worth.

Our worst enemy is not outside the windows of our eyes from which we see, but it's from a dark place deep within that we occasionally keep company with that filters how we see the world, ourselves, and others. In the mirror is a picture of what others see, but in the eyes one can see deeply in one's own heart. One can see the true cause of one's plight. The lack of character and integrity plagues most men, men born to lead yet choose to fall on the sword of their own failures. They take the easy way out by becoming victims of circumstance rather than taking the rough road of fighting one's way to victory. There has never been an enemy to us than the enemy we have been to ourselves, for most of us have failed to realize that true freedom comes from being personally responsible for our own fate and not the whims of man. Value and purpose come from God; and no man, except ourselves, can truly keep us from becoming that which we were created to be which should be our quest. Of course, there may be barriers, but In God's image, all men were created; this means that it is in us to create the world we want to live in. We can choose to be abased or we can choose to abound. The struggle to achieve is different for us all, but the common thread we all have is that of a choice even in the face of insurmountable opposition. Faith, a made-up mind, and a determined heart empowers us to no longer be our own worst enemy but one of our strongest allies. We do not have to look far to find who's responsible for the life we have; none of which can solely be blamed on systems, others, chance or fate; *for within us all is everything we need to destroy ourselves or to develop ourselves into something great.* Greatness can only be achieved in the face of opposition.

12. Putting something together is much harder than taking something apart. Unity requires humility, patience, and understanding; it requires effort. Division is an out-of-control cancer that spreads with little effort; it destroys people, relationships, and everything in its path. It is the rotten fruit of a person's heart, and it is normally carried at the tip of their tongue. Words have power and should always be considered carefully. Through our words, we either put things together, or we tear something apart.

13. I literally did not have any words for today. I even told God that I had nothing to say. I open my devotional up to January 7 and in big, black, bold print were the words "God has something to say." So I said, "Okay what do you have to say?" This is what he put on my heart: "one nation under God [Yahweh]." This phrase is the glue that holds us all together. If we take God out of it, this is what we

will have, "One nation under." If we continue the path we are on, this ship will start sinking; America will go under if there isn't repentance or a return to God. This is not a matter of skin; this is a matter of sin. What you see being played out in our society is all symptoms of the sickness sin. We have to keep our focus on living out the righteousness of Christ in our lives daily before God and each other. We had better learn the lesson of love before we are destroyed by the ignorance of hate.

14. Time is not for waste, but it is for purpose. Everyone is given 24 hours a day, so how come some people "succeed" in life while others don't? The answer to this question is a question. What did we do with the 24 hours we were given? The answer to this question reveals the habits that lead to success or failure.

15. Be a bridge; take no side, but bring each side together. Be the link, the voice of reason in the middle of confusion. If the world demands that we choose a side, we must choose the side of Christ. We must choose the side of love and unification. When it's all said and done, all we have in this life is each other. God made us all dependent, first, on him, and then secondly, upon each other. Together, we can do so much more. The bridge is a place of healing; it's a place of common ground in which we come together for one common goal, and that is to serve the master on this side and the other side!

16. Some people think that there is something wrong with everybody and everything else, not realizing that the problem is within themselves. The problem is their work ethics, their lack of commitment, their lack of following through, their habits, their lack of keeping their word, and their lack of discipline. They blame everyone and everything for the reason why nothing works in their life. If we do not succeed in whatever we set out to do, the blame is the image we see when we look into the mirror.

17. An untrained child is everybody's problem. Disrespect is not cute: it produces menaces to society.

18. Let's get honest here! What is behind the problems we face in the world today? Is it greed? Is it white supremacy? Is it black power? Is it religion? Is it hate? What is it that like the wind we can feel it but can't quite grasp it? The problems we face is the result of the evil that is in the hearts of men. Men are cut from the same cloth and are capable of doing the same things. We can't put a face on evil. We can't even put a color, race, social status, or gender on evil. It's a chameleon in which it has and takes on many different forms. Evil is in us all to do; it is a condition of the flesh. We alone, with the help of the Holy Spirit, control its influence in our actions and in our lives. It steals, it kills, and it destroys. It is merciless and unforgiving to all who cross its path. Like a weed in a garden, it shows up out of nowhere to choke out life. It's always there no matter how much we pluck or pull; it's the reason why bad things happen to good people. Evil is the opposite of good, and without it, we wouldn't know what good is; the same is true about good because without it, we wouldn't know what evil is. The existence of both defines each other. My point is that there is good and evil in us all. Given the right situation, it's in us all to do good and, at the same time, do evil. It is a human condition in which the one we feed the most is the one that comes forth in our lives. Always, give people the benefit of a doubt, for we all deserve a chance to show who we really are in our hearts. To try to put a face, a color, a race, a gender, or a social economic status on either is "like opening a box of chocolates." We never know what we are going to get.

19. Whatever we fear are the things we hate. Fear produces hatred in us, and it is faith that produces love in us.

20. I don't look so much as if a person is black or white; I look for decency in a person.

21. What's in us is bigger than the box others try to put us in. Our character will take us beyond the border of the walls

that limit us if we serve as if we are serving the Lord. When we want more, it requires more and that of ourselves!

22. God created us all to be different; diversity is a God idea. Our differences were not designed to divide us, but they were designed to be a different expression of the beauty of God's creation. If all the birds sang the same songs and everything we see was in black and white, what kind of world would this be? We should celebrate the beauty in everyone and everything! Our differences are what make us special.

23. Wealth never leaves the earth, but it is redistributed to those who harness the knowledge to attract it. Once attracted, it stays with those who possess the wisdom to manage it.

24. It is indeed a jungle out there, and it is the survival of the fittest. The poor, with their poor mentality, beats the same dead horse while the rich borrows the neighbor's horse and rides away. The poor continues to lose while rich continues to win from a material perspective. Should the poor blame the rich for being resourceful, knowledgeable, and disciplined? Can the poor really accuse the rich for being selfish? Is it not the poor who does nothing to take back control of trajectory of their lives? Is it not the poor who complain even about the charity given to them? It's never enough. Is it not the rich who give to these charities to help to those who choose to be less fortunate? Is it not the rich, in their entrepreneur spirit, who create industry that provides jobs for the poor? Now, tell me, who is more selfish? Is this problem created by the rich or the poor? Does the problem come from how some are educated? Is it a systematic or a generational problem? The rich or the poor are not to blame here, only the individual. We all are born with a measure of faith and the capacity to rise above the many obstacles' life will challenge us with. The choice to overcome and succeed is within the individual regardless of their background. The success of millions testifies against those who think otherwise.

25. A cage doesn't take away a bird's ability to fly; it just controls when he can. When we set ourselves free from the cage or limitations of our minds, in time, a decision becomes our only limit.

26. When we know who we are, serving others becomes easier. The deep need for significance and notoriety is expressed through "extreme" expressions. You can always tell a lot of what's going on inside of a person by what's going on outside of them; extreme hairdos and colors, fancy clothes, extravagant homes, expensive cars, tattoos sleeves, weird piercings, provocative clothing, gothic wear, promiscuity, doing anything (I mean anything) for that big promotion, a title, the selling of one's soul to fraternal organizations or gangs no matter the cost, even being gay and so on screams "notice me." It is an outward display of inner insecurities. It screams I want to be important (which is nature but this extremism is different).

    What's sad is when the promise of the power of these things fail, one still has to endure or face that which we all fear—rejection. This person is left surrounded by things yet still unfulfilled. They desperately continue to try to be instead of just being as if being is not enough. There is nothing wrong with being ambitious (God endorses it) with the right motive (for His kingdom and glory), but a pursuit of happiness through accomplishments and self-glory always leads to disappointment. It a vast hole in which the more someone puts into it, the bigger it gets.

    The pursuit of power is empty because it's not true power. The pursuit of acceptance is empty because this desire can't be satisfied except with one exception—Jesus. Our need for acceptance and power has to be satisfied from up above in order to be lasting. Clothes and hairdos go out of styles, cars depreciate, friends and people come and go, homes lose their luster, titles can be taken away, and so on; but having Jesus may not get us acceptance from people, but by having Him, we have everything we need to be okay with ourselves. He fills that void we all have. Jesus is the only thing that can plug that gaping hole that we try to fill so desperately with other things. He does this by erasing self-image and giving us a new image—His image. Dressed in His image, none of that other stuff really matters. We become okay with having stuff not because it defines us. We become okay with not having stuff, as well because we know who and whose we are. Eventually, the opinions of men and the false power of stuff will no longer matter; the only thing that will matter is who matters most, Jesus, and loving what He loves, people.

27. If you are never taught what's right, how will you ever know what's wrong?

28. We always look at things that divide as a subtraction, when in fact, it could mean growth. It is necessary for some things to separate or divide in order to progress to the next level. Whomever we surround ourselves with will impact how far we can go in life. If the people around us are not doing anything with their lives or encouraging us to do something with our lives, they are not our friends. As time passes, we will find that opportunities will slip away from us, and our so-called friends will still be hanging out around the corner of nothing. Also, remember that we can change our environment to better ourselves, but if we don't change the environment in our heads, in time, what we are leaving behind may be drawn to us again.

29. The right time only last for a moment. It is a closing window and a wind that comes and goes without notice. One must be ready at all times to seize the moment when it presents itself. If we are hungry enough, we will eat.

30. If we walk in love, there is nothing anyone can say or do to hurt us. Love covers their misguided actions, and love gives the one walking in it understanding of the deeper issue and compassion on those who lack understanding.

31. If we will allow ourselves to fall in love with the truth, we will never fall in bed with the cheap thrill of a lie.

32. To show up for our children is to let them know that they are not alone in this world. It gives them a sense of strength that empowers them to know that they can do whatever is presented before them, and more importantly, it communicates their value. It shows them that they are loved. The little effort we show may not seem to be much, but it means the world which is more than one could ever know. These moments are eternal and never forgotten.

33. In an environment of secrets are the chains of our pain.

34. He who controls the ideas that influence our thoughts controls us all.

35. Not even poor people are poor all the time; they have access to monies such as $6,000–$8,000 income tax returns, SSI checks, child support payments, money saved from food stamps, money saved from subsidies, government housing, and most Americans can save $20 a week without it being a hardship. It's what being done with the money that keeps poor individuals poor. Seeds are meant to be planted, and that takes discipline and time.

36. As I sat down to read, I realized I left my water bottle on the table across the room. In my mind, I wished it to come by reaching my hand out, but it did not move. I remained thirsty, yet there was water just a few feet from me. Such is in life; wishing for something, without the effort it takes to get it, is just a waste of time. Dreaming of something without an executed plan to get it just means we are still asleep. We have to go after what we want!

37. Poverty is a result of one's habits and is the evidence of one's thinking. Financial peace is not found in how much one makes, but it is in how much one spends. A heart that is never satisfied is surrounded by stuff, but it shall only know emptiness. Futility is its breakfast and vanities are its supper.

38. One group's labor has always produced another group's wealth; racism has never been about color, but it was and still is about power.

39. If we always remember that people are more important than possessions, we will never lose our humanity.

40. Sometimes people get so used to the cage that they were put in that they lose the desire to get out, things we get used to become comfortable, which makes the unknown uncomfortable to the point that some people close, lock, and swallow the key for that which cost them little.

41. At some point, we can fight until the fight becomes ridiculous There is racism. There is sexism. There is classism, and there is political bias. The landscape of this world is full of divisions which demands that individuals choose a side. It matters not whose wrong or right; in the spirit of man, we all fight. We fight with ourselves, and we fight with each other. We fight everyone except our true enemy—the hate.

42. If we have to depend on others to feed us, it very possible that someday we will be hungry.

43. Those who hate are the poorest of all.

44. Submission is not a bad word; it is a word of protection; it was designed for our protection. We should submit to authority, as well to one another; but if that authority is evil, then we should submit to a higher authority which is in God. So why would a person be afraid of something or someone set up for their protection? Could it be that their conscience isn't clear? Could it be that they are not submitted and set on fulfilling the lust of their own evil hearts? If we will police our own actions, we will never have to concern ourselves with being policed. This says it all.

Let every person be subject to the governing authorities. For there is no authority except from God, and those that exist have been instituted by God. Therefore, whoever resists the authorities resists what God has appointed, and those who resist will incur judgment. For rulers are not a terror to good conduct, but to bad. Would you have no fear of the one who is in authority?

Then do what is good, and you will receive his approval, for he is God's servant for your good. But if you do wrong, be afraid, for he does not bear the sword in vain. For he is the servant of God, an avenger who carries out God's wrath on the wrongdoer. Therefore, one must be in subjection, not only to avoid God's wrath but also for the sake of conscience [being a responsible citizen]. (Romans 13:1–5)

That, my friend, is the truth that no one wants to talk about. It is the fattest elephant I've ever seen in a room. Until we are honest about what truly needs to change, nothing will change!

CHAPTER 6

The Season of Fulfillment: The Writing on the Wall

Heavenly Father,

IN THE SPIRIT OF REVIVAL, we petition you to forgive us; for collectively as Americans, we have become more of lovers of pleasure and of ourselves rather than being faithful lovers of you. We have put our confidence in the arm of flesh and have *now* found ourselves as a whole surviving on the respirator of what *used* to be.

The ax is at the root of the tree. Shall not warnings be given, and we be not alarmed? Lord, let us not find ourselves in an even more debased place before we lift up our heads to cry out for revival in our nation and repent of the innocent shed blood of the unborn and others that cry out to you both day and night from the blood-stained soil of America.

Have mercy on us, for America has been lured asleep in a cloud of deception and has lost, for the most part, her discernment of truth and her burden for souls. Revive us from the powerless spiritual condition we have fallen to because of the removal of prayer not just from schools but from our hearts. We ask you this day to resuscitate the spiritually dead and break up the stony hearts of hate with the unfailing power of your love. Father, you are the life support in whom we trust in the midst of these contentious and perilous times. Give us all a new hunger and a new thirst to not just stay in the fight but to lead the charge in representing you to the world.

We are totally dependent upon you for we have learned that we cannot legislate or manufacture revival, for it is only through the inviting of your Holy Spirit that the hearts of men can change. Purge us of iniquity, fix that which is broken in us, restore the gates, and then open our eyes through the awakening of our hearts. May we then discern the times and be your voice in the wilderness crying out for repentance. Then because of the restorative power of your forgiveness and a new sense of urgency in our prayers, like fire, send a wave of revival across this land; for apparently, we have reached a point in which we can no longer manage the barriers of our differences without the "barrier breaking" move of your spirit.

Unify us with the common cause of righteousness for America. Raise up leaders at every level to guard the gates and to take back territory in this country for your kingdom. May the world see more brightly the shining city upon a hill that shines through darkness because of your protective hand and blessing over this land. May they see a beacon of hope with people moving and operating in the power of your glory! Lord, stir us, so that you may find faith in America upon your return! *We want your hand but for such a time as this, we desperately need your face.* Amen.

Now America! We must now come to the end of ourselves, and take heed when we think we stand, lest we fall!"

> Prepare the way for the Lord, make straight
> paths for Him. Every valley shall be filled in, every
> mountain and hill made low. The crooked roads
> shall become straight, the rough ways smooth. And
> all mankind will see God's salvation. (Luke 3:4–6)

This prayer was written in the middle of one of the most contentious summers we have ever had. The summer of the year 2020 was filled with pandemic lockdowns, record job loss, food insecurities, social unrest, racial tension, political swabbing, record death tolls, nature disasters, and church closures all under one pressure cooker just waiting to explode. It was obvious then as it is now that we are a couple of events from everything spiraling dangerously out of control. Our land, this nation, needs a healing; it needs God. The writing is already on the wall, and if we do not turn back to God in this season of time, an even greater judgement will be released. We pray in hopes that it won't take this for God to finally get our attention, but the alarm clock is ringing. Will the warning be heard? Will those who have been asleep awake? Is it already too late? Time and that which is left shall reveal all things.

Of Things to Come and Things that Came

In December 2019, I had this overwhelming feeling that the year 2020 would be eye opening, and we would no longer just see the tip of the iceberg but we would see that which has been hidden. How little did I know of the things that were coming and yet are still to come? These are the words I spoke that day,

> This shall be a contentious year to say the least. 2020 is the year that we will begin to see more clearly of the things going on behind the scenes. The veil of this realm shall split and reveal things we thought were coming but are already here. We are on the brink of seeing that which has been spoken. The plan of God is unfolding before our eyes. The blind will now see the hidden things and once again be faced with a choice to accept or reject; to obey or rebel. This is our turning point; this is the year of the seeing. The blind will have a choice to see or remain blind groping in their ignorance or darkness. To see and embrace truth is revelation, but to be blind is to have become one with a lie—to be deceived; a deception that leads to destruction. Many will choose to see through the window that 2020 will provide while others will simply close their eyes unto their own destruction. Let us focus on truth so that we will avoid the great deception that is here and is coming!

Who would have believed that we would have had a year like the year we had in 2020? March 13, 2020, marked a dramatic change in America in which left us all with a sense that life would never be the same again. The world was in crisis. At the same time, America was crippled by a pandemic, called COVID-19, and reeling from issues involving economics, protest, violence and looting, political turmoil, social media fights about race, divisiveness, quarantine, church and school closures, record deaths, fear and uncertainty, presidential campaigns, record unemployment, businesses closing for good, China's sanctions and fall out, asteroids nearly missing the earth, the sun showing concerning signs, and locust spreading across the world. The one thing that has been so surprising is the division and hate because tragedies normally bring people together but not this time—not in this season.

On December 31, 2020, I sensed a message for 2021 that was woven into 2020. I felt that 2020 was going to bleed over into 2021, but there were going to be major shifts that will once again cause a shaking much like the aftershocks caused by an earthquake. Year 2020 and 2021 would be like two tectonic plates rubbing against each other. Those things or people that are not strong enough will fall, but those built to resist the shifting shall remain. Here is the message:

> The end of something always means the beginning of something else. In the rear-view mirror of what was, we look forward and wonder what will be. Will this year prove better than the last? What will we lose, and what shall we gain? What will be different, and what shall remain? What's up ahead? no one truly knows, but faith gives us hope through the highs and the lows.
>
> In 2020, our eyes were open and all could see clearly the choices and consequences before us. Now, I believe in 2021, we will begin to see the start of something big being completed (7+7+7=21). I believe 2021 will be a year of Transformation! I believe we will see great change

like we have never seen in modern times. Time is not winding down rather it's coming into its fullness. Based on the Jewish calendar 5781, There will be a strong appeal by God for repentance (read psalm 81) as we now understand how fragile life and everything can be. Fear not! May this year be that of victory for you in the spirit! Do not let fear stand in the place where faith has been in your life. Don't be shaken by the things 2020 has allowed you to see, but allow the experience to equip you and reinforce you for the times that shall be. Remain sober and continue to watch and pray!

Now, I do not claim to be a prophet; but of course, you don't have to be one to discern that something big is just around the corner. Elements of biblical prophecies seem to all be converging at once, and the atmosphere of the earth seem to be growing darker by the hour. Of course, the darker it is, the brighter the light of Christ will shine in us and through us. It will penetrate the blindness of darkness; this light in darkness will also draw attention to us in the form of Christian persecution. That, my friend, is right around the corner; in fact, it has already started with the ordering of governments to shut down places of worship due to the COVID-19 pandemic. According to Hebrews 10:25, we should not forsake the assembling of ourselves, but we should exhort each other even more so as we see the day approaching. The closing of houses of worship will naturally lead to more darkness. *In His mercy, God has given men time for the purpose of repentance.* Time does run out eventually and then comes His righteous judgement.

The Ink Is Drying

The night has slowly fallen upon us; we are approaching our darkest hour. We have taken the sacred things of God (Yahweh) and unrepentantly used them to fulfill every lustful pleasure. In every area of society, there has been efforts to push God out and replace Him with idols and false gods. As a result, every root or solid thing is being pulled up. The seams are being unraveled; and the foundations, which has been our security, has been cracked. The very ground on which we stand has shifted and has caused everything that has been built to be compromised. Sin has a way of eroding us from underneath before there is any sign of it on the surface. We must take heed when we think we stand, lest we fall. There are warning signs all around us. Each sign is a letter of the writing that's on the wall. The atmosphere is not normal, and the times are indeed troubling. The season has changed. The ground beneath our feet has loosened; the things we have put our faith in, besides God (Yahweh), are now showing the true nature of their ability to save us.

We should never put our faith in something to save us that, in fact, needs saving itself. I have seen jobs disappear because there was no money to bail them out. I've seen bank accounts emptied because of no income and crops destroyed because of no rain, or even worse, locust. I've seen million-dollar homes succumb to wildfires, as in vain, the owners had to drop their water hoses and run to safety. I've seen people in flood waters carrying their wooden gods to safety; I have also seen them feeding them even though they wouldn't be fed. What kind of foolish is this? Our only hope is in God (Yahweh) and what he gave us in His Son (Jesus) to reconcile us unto Himself; so if darkness shall come, let it come for what power does darkness have over the light. This is our moment as the church (the bride of Jesus Christ) to shine ever so brightly that everyone can see the glory of our God (Yahweh). The world needs and will need an answer, and only the truth will satisfy when their hunger for understanding is greater than their hunger for their lust. The light must shine at all times, for some (lost people) shall find their way through the darkness.

The world, as we know it, has changed dramatically in one year. This change is like no change we have seen because all of a sudden, the signs that are biblical and prophetic seem to all be converging at once. Historic wildfires, unprecedented hurricane season, tension with China and Russia, highly contagious viruses, riots over social justice, lawlessness, civil unrest, increase in the murder rate and violent crimes, churches being forced to stop assembling and singing their praises to God, Israel signing historic agreements with Muslim countries, which is believed to be the first steps to the rebuilding of the third temple in Jerusalem, Pope Francis calling for interfaith prayer where each leader prays to his own god, socialism and Marxist ideas gaining popularity, swarm of locust eating the crops of farmers cause famine to spread, sex trafficking of women and children, the increase of homosexuality ideation as being moral and acceptable, the rise of suicide and drug abuse, financial collapse of nations, and the killing of unborn innocent just to name a few things. This world is headed for a reset; something has to give because the track we are on will provoke God to finally put an end to it all.

> And then shall many be offended, and shall
> betray one another, and shall hate one another.
> (Matthew 24:10)

We are living in times were elephants (Republicans) and donkeys (Democrats) seem to be more important than the Lamb of God (Jesus). Neither the elephant nor the donkey has a heaven to put us in but has created hell on earth for us to live in today. The media is supposed to mediate, but instead they have turned the followers of the elephant and donkey against each other. In the fighting, we have forgotten about the sacrifice of the Lamb. Respect seems to be a thing of the past, but those of us who claim Christ should soften our hearts when it comes to our political stance. With a hard heart, it is next to impossible to change anyone's mind or stance. People just do not care about our correction until they know that we genuinely care about them. We may not agree with what the other person believes or stands for, but we must not forget that on the other side of our indignation is another person with a God-given soul. If their stance is wrong, we must still remember that God loves them just as much as he loves us in our "righteous" stance. It's just like two of our own kids fighting. We can clearly see whose wrong or right; we can clearly see where both have faults. We can clearly see the solution, but because each child is so dug in, they can't see it.

The solution is loving thy neighbor as thyself. Love is patient, and it is kind. It keeps no record of wrong, and it covers and so on. Where is the compassion for hurting people? *Where is the humility that reconcile relationships instead of the pride that inherently divides?* Where is civility, and where is common decency? Where are the peacemakers that shall inherit the kingdom of God? Where are the voices of reason and unity? Where are the parents that should have whooped our butts, thereby teaching us right from wrong and respect for authority? Where is the leadership that should be our example of what being a fellow American, human being, brother, sister, or Christian is about? Where are we as a country, and at the rate we are going, where will we be in the future? Are we so angry that we can't feel what we are doing to this nation and to ourselves? Are we so hopeless that rather than taking personal responsibility, we must blame others BEFORE we take a look in the mirror? Are we so fearful that we have lost our faith? Are we so distracted that we don't even notice our decline morally, spiritually, economically (27 trillion in debt at the end of 2020) and as a world power? Are we so numb that we can politicize a mask and not even seem to be shaken by the number of deaths due to an invisible enemy (COVID-19)? May I submit to you that there is more than one invisible enemy at work here (both physical and spiritual). Are we so blind that we can't see that our children are watching and learning hate and rebellion from us? In the years to come, what will they reap from what we have sown? Are we so spiritually dead that we have lost our conscience because we can't hear the voice of God? Do we value our cause more than His cause and our voice more than His voice? In our actions, do we dare raise our voice at God?

Don't make your political stance be your last stance. The lack of love and bad behavior makes it is very difficult for either side to hear what needs to be said and heard. Without love, there is no power to change anything; our voices will sound like Charlie Brown's teacher, and only we will understand what we are trying say. We will demonstrate, protest, march, and use words; yet none of these will have the power to prick and change harden hearts. We will continue to talk, but never come to any lasting solutions. We should stand for all people and not just our own. We should stand for righteousness and not just a party. We should stand for Christ and not the idols we have created. We should stand for justice and not for revenge or guilt but because it's right. We should stand only once we have been on our knees so that we will be conscious of and able to articulate what we are standing for. Always remember that one day, we will stand before God and give an account for the attitude of our hearts, our behavior, our comments, our actions, our faith or lack thereof. We shouldn't focus on being an elephant or a donkey, for we are more than just mere animals (even though some of us have been acting like animals). We should be citizens of the kingdom of God who just happens to be Americans, and if we can't be that, we should at least try to be decent.

> And Jesus answered and said unto them, take heed that no man deceives you. (Matthew 24:4)

Most news media outlets these days seem to mediate in error between what is actually happening and what they want to see happen. They seem to sensationalize stories by taking so many things out of its full contexts. They rewrite the story by taking parts of the truth and piecing things together to fit the agenda of those keeping them on the air. They select anchors and attract viewers that support their views. So the media we put so much faith in to tell us the unbiased truth is being controlled by "the wizard of Oz" for all we know. They have become snake charmers (there are many godly media outlets and anchors out there); but the ones I'm talking about play and wave the flute which causes vibrations that have negative impacts in our cities, our communities, and the world. Those snakes, those who have poor hearing and sight, are controlled by the tunes that are played. The vibrations or waves were created by the narrative written to prop up pre-established agendas to control the emotions and belief systems of the masses. Whoever controls a person's thought life, controls them, and this is the potential power of the media. These days you can almost tell what news someone watches by what they say (almost as being brainwashed). Their speech betrays them because it reveals the contents of their heart. We can tell who spends more time in the Word of God rather than in the elements of the media that operates in witchcraft. Several media outlets use slander, fear, control, lies, and occasionally, after vomiting on us, a good story.

Now, I'm one who believes in watching the news, good or bad, to a certain extent. I limit my time in the news, but I'm not going to hide my head in a hole and be so ignorant I can't hold a current event conversation with someone. One of the greatest ways to defeat an enemy is the know the enemy. Know his playbook, and know what he is up to. We should be selective in what we eat, but know what's on and under the table. We should watch out for the bite of the snake once the flute has been played because it will cause us to hate and not even know why we hate. Without the influence of Christ, we are like sheep that follow whomever has the biggest stick, the loudest voice, and oddly enough, for no other reason, those who look like us instead of a true shepherd. We tend to not think for ourselves, but we go right along to the slaughterhouse because it's well followed or it seems popular. We should avoid being dumb sheep; know what's on the table (and in the Bible). If we remain sober and stay close to the Good Shepherd (Jesus) for in the high grass (hidden agendas or places you can't see) "lies" the snake.

Am I calling everyone influenced by the media snakes? No, I'm saying that the flute(media) has a way to get a rise out of us. I'm saying that there is a snake who speaks to us (if we allow him) that, if not filtered through the truth which is the Word of God, will lure us by the lust of our own flesh (greedy, selfish, reckless, stubborn, and even religious sheep who think they do but don't even know Jesus the good shepherd). It is so subtle in how the serpent uses a little truth (it's camouflage) to conceal demonized agendas to remove our protection Christ Jesus and try to erase Him from our society; that's the snake charmer's agenda and that's the fruit he wants us to bite, a godless society full of hate, unforgiveness, destruction, immorality, murders, fears, wars, division, and chaos. The media plays the flute; the people take on the snakes' reptilian ways (survival of the fittest) and dance to the sound of its tune in our streets, in our homes, in our speech, in our beliefs, in our politics, in our actions, in our minds, in our schools, and even in our places of worship. As the flute plays, we close our eyes and are drawn so far from God that when the music stops, it's too late because that which distracted us has now consumed us. This is a form of worshiping the beast. This anti-Christ spirit seeks control of our minds. His goal is to use us to destroy us by replacing God through the erecting of idols in our hearts and through the becoming of a god unto ourselves. If not sober, we began calling that which is immoral moral, that which is corrupt righteous, that which is good bad, that which is pure impure, that which is evil our rights, that which is right wrong, and that which is God out of date.

And because iniquity shall abound, the love
of many shall wax cold. (Matthew 24:12)

Who gave us the right to kill the unborn, the elderly (assisting suicides), or each other? Who gave us the right to redefine marriage and God-given genders? Instead of changing sexual orientation, we need to re-orient ourselves back to God. Who gave us the right to hate a person, not for his or her level of decency but simply for the color of his or her skin? Who gave us the right to enslave others for our own selfish gain or to enslave others, drug, and sell for sex? Who gave us the right to engage or watch inappropriate relationship with children? Who gave us the right to twist the gospel and bring abominations in the house of God. *Jesus wants us to come just as we are, but He never intended on being tolerant of our sin and leaving us how we came.* Who gave us a right not to preach and live the cross? My friend, it wasn't the creator; it was the serpent who lied to us by twisting what God said. He gave us the fruit God, for our own protection, said we shouldn't eat. This snake knew how to mediate (speak for someone) and twist the story (just like the media) in such a way that would feed into our own desires. He knew how to deceive us. Wake up! This serpent wants to replace God, who should be the object of our worship, with his own image (to look and act like him). Many of us blindly fall for the trappings of seemingly righteous causes, but if the cause is rooted in unrighteousness, then that cause shall bring a curse. We stand in crowds full of rebellion against authority with our fist in sky to a God that, with one word, could wipe us off the face of the earth. Where is the fear of the Lord? Do we dear burn Bibles in the streets of America? "Vengeance is mine, said the Lord." He shall judge us all, and we better have Jesus as our defense. Sin causes us to literally lose our minds and eventually our souls. Pride has so taken the place of humility before God and the things of God that hearts, just as Pharaoh of Egypt who stubbornly destroyed his people and himself, have become hardened. A stony heart has no life flowing through it. *A person who rejects God is already dead waiting on time to catch up, yet without knowing it.* In their blindness, they are unable to see or hear the warning signs.

According to a recent Gallup survey, only 29 percent of Americans believe that "it is very important for couples who have children together to be married." Marriage is one of the oldest institutions designed by God on earth. It is the bedrock or foundation of human civilization; it is the incubator for raising stable, well-balanced children. This ideological percentage in this survey is a steep decline in the value and purpose of marriage in the eyes of Americans. We are witnessing the desecration of marriage which means to use the sanctity of marriage for something it was not purposed for. We have progressive leaders who would try to erase the gender differences created by God within marriage. House speaker Nancy Pelosi and Democratic congressman James McGovern announced a set of changes to the house rules to enshrine what they call gender-inclusive language which cause for stopping the use of so-called non-inclusive words. They proposed to strike the use of words including father, mother, son, daughter, aunt, uncle, husband, and wife. This is only the start of what progressives will do to move our nation closer and closer toward a godless society as a whole. Every character in a story has a role, and those roles are filled with purpose. Without the roles, there is no purpose. A character or life without purpose is as lost as one groping in a dark room. Life will eventually have no meaning if roles are erased.

The reality that's been our problem since the beginning of time is that people, without the knowledge of the truth, want to govern themselves or be the god of themselves. The heart of man, compromised with greed, desires to rule others and to answer only to himself. According to Psalm 33:12, "Blessed is the nation whose God is the Lord," so how blessed can we be if we put the god of self above God? How blessed can a nation be who tries to erase the Lord and yield to the darkness that plagues our society? How blessed are a people who know truth, yet they hide their heads in holes because they are just avoiding the darkness and waiting on Jesus? Did not Jesus say occupy until I come? I'm reminded of a quote from Edmund Burke which states, "The only thing necessary for the triumph of evil is for good men to do nothing." With the territory and the authority God has given us, we have a responsibility to hold back the full force of evil as long as we can and advance His kingdom in the earth. Why? Because souls are hanging in the balance.

God's Holy Spirit in us (the church) is the restrainer of evil in the world. This little light of ours must shine and not be hid under a bushel. "No man, when he hath lighted a candle, putteth it in a secret place, neither under a bushel, but on a candlestick, that they which come in may see the light" (Luke 11:33). As the days grow darker, the brighter the light within us will become. This brightness will lead to the persecution of those who carry the light because light is in direct opposition to darkness, and darkness hates the light. The fighting and confusion we see every day seems natural, but it is spiritual in nature. It is so subtle that even some who claim Christianity will be and have already been seduced by hatred or by the festering wounds they carry that they are blinded and enticed by the devil himself. If someone touches a wound that has not fully healed, it can be re-injured and the pain of it be replayed over and over, causing reactions of defensive behavior. Seeds of unforgiveness are planted, and when they are full grown, it's harvested (gathered) and given (mostly through the media or a medium) to others to feast on. This poison goes straight to the heart causing blindness, confusion, delusion, division, anger, hopelessness, rebellion, resentment, and hatred.

Racism is something the true enemy (Satan) uses to hook people to demonized causes. He baits the hook and unassuming people like fish take the bait only to someday end up in the proverbial "frying pan" to be feasted on by the one who set the trap. We should stay away from the shiny attractive things (popular but ungodly causes) because underneath them are hooks designed for our jaws which will pull us toward our own captivity and destruction. The only good and curse-free cause is the causes led by Christ. If God doesn't accept it, we shouldn't accept it. If God is not tolerant of it, we should not be tolerant of it. If God is for it, we should be for it; and if He is against, we should be against it.

To Stand For

We should examine closely the causes we take up. Are they rooted and grounded in the Word of God? I've examined myself: I'm against the murder of the unborn or the shedding of any "innocent" blood. I'm against white supremacy, black power, and all hate groups and organizations because hate is not of God. I'm against the homosexual agenda (God reserved the rights to His design, and we shouldn't infringe upon that) which is an agenda that will lead to Christian persecution, and I'm against appointing people to places of authority whose sole agenda is to change or modify laws to support abominations, thereby rejecting God.

I'm for the return of our nation to being solely governed by godly principles because according to Proverbs 13:34, "Righteousness makes a nation great, but sin diminishes any people." I'm for a government that supports and is a friend to Israel (God promised to bless us). I'm for men working and earning a living (I've always been told that if I didn't work, I wouldn't eat; social programs should only be for those who truly need a hand up and not a hand out because handouts enslave people); we must be law-abiding and take personal responsibility for our lives and actions. I'm for completely enforcing our laws, but as our God does, we must create ways to show mercy. Law without mercy dooms us all. *I'm for second chances if a person repents and tries to do better. We should do everything we can to help them because if they are better, we all are better.* I'm for job creating policies and fair trade. I'm for acknowledging and addressing some of the environmental concerns but not for paying the whole bill for the world. We are managers of this earth that has been given to us. We should be balanced in our efforts to preserve the resources we have been given and be good stewards. I'm for those who enforce the laws designed to promote peace and a safe society. I'm for obeying laws and not rebelling against authority, order, and civility. If everyone would police themselves and their own hearts, there wouldn't be a need to be policed.

I'm for conservatism in government, laws, and Supreme Court justices; I'm also for economic and social conservatism. I'm for restrictions on drug legalization because a drugged nation will lead to a cursed and bewitched people. I'm for criminal justice and policing reforms, but God is the only one who can truly reform the hearts of men. We need more of Him than anything else because the issue of our plight is simply the heart. I'm for interpreting the Bible and the constitution (not to put the constitution on the same level as the Bible) as is and not adding to it or taking away from it. *Foundational truths transcend generations and works to hold everything, that is, together.* Without these ancient foundational truths, every- thing we know and have built will began to unravel and descend into the chaos of disorder. In spite of man's valiant efforts, God is truly the only one that can govern a people; and in the end, it is God who will righteously govern the earth when His kingdom comes and His will be done. But for now, I'm for reforming anything that isn't work- ing to make us better and pointing us to the original intent of His purpose. More than anything, I'm for reforming families by pushing an agenda for them to return to God by acknowledging Him in our schools and in every area of our society. If this were to happen, many of the social ills we have would be no more.

It's not so much the men, which are distractions to what is really happening in the spirit realm, we will vote for as presidents because they are severely flawed (as we all are, they are just representations of what we have become as a whole), but it is the agendas and principles we vote for that will determine the future of the soul of this great nation and not the men. We must take for Christ whatever ground that is left for the taking. We can either destroy ourselves within and not realize it before it's too late (that's what sin does), or we can return to God with our ideals and values. We all value different things, but it is eternally important that our values align with the agenda and principles of God and not that of our own.

Regardless of what we see in this world, His (God) will shall be done on earth as it is in heaven. Whether we choose His will or our own, the choice is each individual to make. Not to use our voices and authority as kingdom people given to us by God (to be silent) gives up more ground to darkness as they use their voices and push their godless agendas. Some of us may say, "What does it matter? The outcome will be the same anyway!" May I submit that it matters to God for if we stand for His Son, His Son shall stand for us when it matters most. We are men riddled with flaws, yet somehow, God still uses us for His purpose. There is still hope; and now is not the time to give up, shrink back, be silent, or be missing in action. We have a choice to be victorious in this hour by honoring God by standing for His principles in this nation before the world, or we have a choice to reject the principles of God and separate ourselves from God's protection and blessings. The choice (a gift from God that even the angels marvel at) has always been ours as it is now, and so shall it be in the end.

Now What?

Will religious freedoms be taken away? Will we be taxed into poverty? Will the stock market collapse due to shutdowns, bad trade deals, and progressive policies? Will boys get to go to bathrooms with little girls? Will cross-dressers be motivational speakers in our schools? Will the slaughter and sacrifice of the unborn continue? Will our police departments be castrated? Will violence and murder run rampant through our communities? Will history be lost and be rewritten so it's less offensive? Will Marxism and communistic ideology decimate our constitution? Will foreign enemies slip through our borders and rage war from the inside out? Will we turn our backs on Israel and forfeit God's blessing? Will our health-care system become socialized and bankrupted? Will the Supreme Court be packed? Will it be compromised, causing a loss of balance in the three branches of government? Will the divide grow deeper and racism wax worse? Will drug addictions and overdoses grow due to the legalization of marijuana nationally? Will drug lords take over our streets and a generation? Will America be too high to care? Will the national debt continue to rise as we continue to print money with no gold to back it or plan to repay? Will the dollar lose its value and inflation strip us of what little we have left? Will communism fill this void? Will socialism be the last nail in the coffin? Will suicide spike because the lack of jobs and hopeless? Will parents terminate pregnancies because they are unable to feed another mouth? Will China own more real estate here? Will judgement cause extreme weather and earthquakes never before seen strike us to get our attention to no avail? Will we heed the warning and be saved? Will pestilence and pandemics continue to be the news of the day? Will America need foreign aid instead of giving foreign aid? Will our enemies bully us and dare us to fight back? Will the home of the brave turn into the home of the slaves?

"We the people" collectively have made our choice (progressivism). Things could get really bad if in our pride, we reject God, go our own way, and forfeit His blessing over this land. Only time will provide an answer to all of these questions. As for me and my house, no one will make a choice for us; we choose to serve the Lord come what may. For Christ we live, and for Christ we are willing to die. Now that is a sobering reality. Is what we do a religious exercise, or do we truly believe what we say we believe? Selah.

Now what? What do we do? Do we just sit here and watch the sun go down? Do we just wait for the dark clouds to cover our nation? God forbids! God still sits on the throne. God spared total destruction of Sodom and Gomorrah, probably one of the wicked cities ever, as long as the righteous were there. Once they were removed, those cities were destroyed for their wickedness.

We have reached a critical juncture in our existence, and now is not the time to go back to business as usually. If the Lord tarry, we must occupy until He comes! As the darkness arises, so should the light on the inside of us. But how? Remain grounded in the Word of God by reading and studying His Word more. We are entering a season of deception, and the Word will keep us anchored and from drifting off. Many will be carried away desensitized to our increasing growing perverse society. We must stand on His Word even if we have to stand alone. We must keep in mind that being a light in dark places makes us a target. We must expect persecution because people will hate us because of the light or truth we carry that illuminates their error. We might even be labeled as domestic terrorists or a hate group for our lack of tolerance for lifestyles of sin. "Let us hold fast the confession of our hope without wavering, for he who promised is faithful. And let us consider how to stir up one another to love and good works, not forsaking the assembling of ourselves together, as the manner of some is; but exhorting one another: and so much the more, as ye see the day approaching" (Hebrew 10:23–25). We must encourage one another to keep the faith; love and be faithful to God and one another; this is how the world will know that we are truly His disciples. We must share your light (the truth) to all that will listen for those who live in the dark, deep down, are lonely, scared, hopeless, hurting, blind, confused, and condemned. Their hearts whisper to them that they need something more than the empty promises that a sinful lifestyle gives. They know that there has got to be more to life and that the things that are happening in life are not just mere coincidence. We all have a measure of faith to believe for something more. When the world comes to us for an answer, we must be ready in season and out of season as expressed in these scriptures:

> You are the salt of the earth. But if the salt loses its saltiness, how can it be made salty again? It is no longer good for anything, except to be thrown out and trampled underfoot. You are the light of the world. A town built on a hill cannot be hidden. Neither do people light a lamp and

put it under a bowl. Instead they put it on its stand, and it gives light to everyone in the house. In the same way, let your light shine before others, that they may see your good deeds and glorify your Father in heaven. Be the remnant of what was and what shall be. (Matthew 5:13–16)

We have to participate in this government system, but as citizens of another kingdom (believers in the Lord Jesus Christ), we are governed by God and acting as agents to complete the mission given to us. We are ambassadors of heaven representing God's interests in the earth. *These should be exciting times and not fearful times for the believers. We have hope beyond the chaos that is unfolding and that is yet to unfold on the earth.* Time reveals all things, and in time, we all will understand that the fight is not against each other; it's much deeper! We are just caught in the middle of a fight that began before our beginning. This fight has always been over our souls. It's not about political parties, race, or flesh and blood! Against Satan, this fight is the Lord's!

Selah 6:1–44

1. "There are some difficult days ahead," words stated by the late Dr. Martin Luther King Jr. The sins of our nation are great. No man is our messiah; there is only Jesus Christ.

   So regardless of our political persuasion or our ethnic affiliation, if there has ever been a time to pray for the hearts of our leaders (old and new), it is now. If there has ever been a time to humble ourselves before God, it is now. If there has ever been a time to seek His face, it is now. If there has ever been a time we need to trust that God is God and He knows exactly what He's doing, it is now. If there has ever been a time that we need to search our hearts and make sure we are right with God, it is now. If there has ever been a time to recommit ourselves to prayer and devotion to the Lord, it is now. If there has ever been a time that we need to place our hope in Yahweh for our future, it is now. The fight is not ours, but it is the Lord's; we need only to be still and watch the salvation of our Lord. These are great and terrible times—an exciting time for those who know the end of this story. We are here because we were born for such a time. This will be our purification, not to turn away but a time to turn to Him. No matter how dark it gets, the Son of God always shines through! "And we know that *all things work together for good* to them that love God, to them who are the called according to his purpose" (Romans 8:28). If there has ever been a time we need healing, it is now. In this moment, right now, let us forgive each other, and ask the God who knows the secrets our hearts to forgive us.

Father, you have our attention! May your will be done on earth as it is in heaven. May your joy be our strength; please remember the righteousness (through Christ) in America. Please once again bless America (us).

2. The subject below is sensitive and may be offensive to some. It is for certain not politically correct, but it is biblically correct. This truth is like alcohol; it may hurt a lot before there is evidence of healing. It is not my intention to hurt anybody or any group. As a Christian, I'm obligated to love everyone; but as my Father in heaven, I hate sin and what it does to people. I hate it in my own life, and I strive daily to keep it out of my life. Nevertheless, truth must be spoken regardless of who it may offend because without truth, we will fall for and believe in every lie we are told. There is no my truth or your truth; there is only the truth, which is found in the Word of God, given to us out of love. We shouldn't reject love because it will never lie to us. We can trust someone who truly loves us because they will be willing to give up their life for us. If we can't handle the truth or someone loving us with the truth, we may find this offensive and may not need to read any further. This is a large pill to swallow, but if we endure it, it shall release something in the climate in which we all need. The

purpose of this is to awaken those who are sleeping so that they may see with their spiritual eyes the agenda of Satan (the things that are coming). This is not to bash a group but to use truth as an instrument of love to convict hearts and save souls. This is love and not hate.

Well, it seems as though the devil is no longer hiding; he has come out of the closet and is boldly showing his naked self to the world. Who would have thought that there would be people out there, inspired by demons, who would advocate for pedophiles not to be punished or discouraged for their actions because their attraction to kids is a result of their sexual orientation (https://www.snopes.com/fact-check/tedx-pedophilia-sexual-orientation/). They argue that pedophiles have done no wrong because it's biological. They claim that they were born that way. Now, where have we heard this lie before? This lie is from the very pits of hell. They have done plenty wrong because their lust for children has fueled the kidnapping and selling of children for sex. They have done wrong if they touch someone's child only to send that child on a path of promiscuity, sexual perversion, drug abuse, depression, and even suicide. The child porn industry has illegally profited off the exploitation and abuse of children, and now they want to make it okay because it is their sexual orientation! Even the people we esteem such as Hollywood stars, musicians, and athletes has participated in such fetishes. We live in a world now, despite warnings from God, that feels as though we have a right to be and do as we want. Nothing good comes from lawlessness and lasciviousness.

We have been slowly conditioned to the pornography in movies and the music of our day that some conditioned minds may go right along with this crime against humanity. The flood gates of hell have been opened, starting with the gay and lesbian agenda, which is now being pushed in our schools to children to be accepted as normal or natural behavior. They want cross-dressers and transgender individuals to read *My Husband Betty* to our innocent children in classrooms. We can't pray in schools, but we can introduce them to alternative lifestyles. Oh, the irony! According to Romans 1: 27–28 in the Bible, unnatural affections goes against nature and produces nothing but godlessness and broken people. The same goes for unmarried heterosexuals who engage in promiscuity and fornication. Sexual sins not only cause us to sin against God but our own bodies as well. If a generation is taught that it's normal and acceptable, it will become as such, as well as all of the penalties that comes with it according to the Bible. I said ten years ago that perversion (love in reverse) wouldn't stop at the gay and lesbian movement which, in America, changed the God-given definition of marriage; "well, everybody has a right to love who they want to love." There is no love without God, for He is love. He is the very definition of love. He is the creator, and according to Him, marriage is between a man and a woman. I said just ten years ago that the agenda of those who would try to change the definition of marriage would pave the way for pedophiles to be just an alternative lifestyle, and here we are.

Perversion (to use sex for something other than what God intended it's used to be) is a downward spiral, and it won't stop at pedophilia: sex and marriage to animals, incest, father-and-daughter marriages, mother-and-son marriages, and as well as group marriages. Oh, you don't believe me. Well, it has already started with a brother and sister seeking the right to marry in the United States. There is no end to the depravity of men who have turned their back on God. *Left to ourselves, who needs the devil to destroy us, we are very capable of doing it to ourselves.* We, who know truth, must never sanction or align ourselves with these lifestyles in our society. These lifestyles (sins against God or abominations) will and is eroding our society. Every ancient great society eventually was destroyed from the inside out because of how these sins weaken society through the eroding of the family unit. A nation is only as strong as the families that make up that nation. If we destroy the family unit; we weaken the people. There is no clearer evidence of this truth than the American system of African slavery. As a nation, even though it has been around 155 years ago, still has not fully recovered from the demonized strategy of destroying families to weaken, control, and enslave a people. To yield to such sexual perversion in our society will, in turn, make us slaves to an enemy whose sole goal is our destruction. To yield to the normalization of alternative lifestyles comes with spiritual judgements and curses that manifest naturally. We can expect trouble in the flesh such as disease, mental and emotional issues, suicides, violence, drug abuse, murder, self-hate, and hopelessness.

Sexual sins do not just have spiritual consequences; The First Epistle to the Corinthians 6:18 warns of negative physical consequences to sexual sin, a desecration of the Holy Temple, our bodies, which houses the Holy Spirit: "Flee from sexual immorality. All other sins a person commits are outside the body, but whoever sins sexually, sins against their own body." This sin creates soul ties and warps every area of an individual's life, as well as our society. The societies of Sodom and Gomorrah no longer exist; could this be the reason why America is not clearly mentioned in biblical prophecy as a champion for the Lord and a refuge for persecuted believers? The silence on this matter could be an indication of the downfall and our inability as a nation to be the moral voice and leader of this world.

Nevertheless, there is hope for those who remain untainted by the perverse culture; they will someday be persecuted for being the light that uncovers darkness. Their very presence will be a reproach to those in darkness, and they shall be despised for it. It's like turning on the light when someone is sleeping; it definitely will never be appreciated, at least at first for some. The Word of God is not to control or condemn people; it is for our protection. It is a mirror that shows how close or far away our hearts are to or from God's will. A marriage blessed by God is an incubator designed to build balanced lives and a strong and prosperous society. Appropriate relationship were designed by the creator; their purpose was, is, and will always be for releasing blessings and to guard us from the curse. We must stand for the truth even in the face of persecution, for we are not alone. For those who endure to the end, they shall receive the promise of their reward! *We must always remember to love everyone as our Heavenly Father does, but also love them enough to tell them, not from a position of self-righteousness, the truth in love.* As sheep sent out in the midst of wolves, be wise as serpents but as harmless as doves (Matthew 10:16).

3. A global problem attracts a global solution. Waves of difficulty will be a common theme we see played out on the world scene because of the perversion that persist in our culture. The madness of this world has caused God to allow the world to be put on pause or a timeout, if you will, a time of reflection and a time of remembrance. Everything in life has come to a boiling point which is propelling us toward the climatic end foretold. The end is in sight, and time to many is no longer an ally. As we are forced to go in to hiding, we are faced with the reality that we cannot hide from ourselves. We have been granted a pause, time to think about where we've been, where we are, and where we are going.

    COVID-19 has caused us to focus on death, but there is an even more sinister virus we should be concerned about called sin. It is very contagious and has infected people in every corner of the earth. It has been spreading since the beginning of time. This virus leads to death (separation from God), and the only vaccine or cure for it is the blood of Jesus which has all of the antibodies (anti-flesh) we need. The number one cause of death (a separation) in all communities regardless of underlying conditions is sin.

Many will reject this cure to their own demise. Many will social distance themselves from God and isolate themselves with the enemy whose only goal is to destroy them. These same people will try to reason with time, but time is unreasonable. Those that think they have plenty of time shall someday find out that it's too late. "The end of all things is at hand" is a statement that causes some to say, "Yea, they have been saying that for over 2,000 years." Please let me enlighten you. The end of all things for us could happen today; don't get caught unprepared or uncovered with the blood of Jesus.

Warnings are sounding as trumpets all around us. We should be alarmed; we should wake up and see that which is behind what we think we see. A call for repentance is daily being sounded; repent (change/turn toward the Lord), the kingdom of God is at hand! Year 2020 is the beginning of all things coming into focus. When all of the pieces finally come together, the promise of His return shall be fulfilled. Return to He who loved us first before He returns and find us without love—without Him in our hearts. For such a time as this have we been created. We already have what we need to weather the coming storms, a promise. Like time, we must keep moving forward. May the joy of the Lord be our strength.

4. Greed and pride can turn good men to devils. The hunger in man for things rather than God can cause men to turn on and devour each other. This spirit causes pastors to be in competition with each other and churches and its members to be at odds with each other in spite of claiming to serve the same God and having the same spirit. As a result, buildings fill up with backbiters and people feasting on the failures of others. Hearts rejoicing in gossip, instead of praying for the souls affected by a common enemy. The house has been divided, and woe to those who participate in such doings. These are those who think they do the will of the Father, yet deception has covered their heads like a thick veil caus-

ing blindness. They walk around groping under the cover of darkness, falling deeper and deeper into the grips of this deception; they worship, yet the object of their worship is flesh. They pray, yet it sounds more like a wish list to satisfy their lust rather than a prayer that touches heaven about this generation, our leaders, repentance, forgiveness, thankfulness, revival, the body of Christ, and souls. Beware for deception is coming! Our convenience and comforts have consumed our hearts, leaving the value and sanity of every human being's life to God as an afterthought. Our gatherings have become centers that entertain people into hell as we refuse to preach the cross and the bloody truth of the gospel. Everyone is sensitive these days and easily offended but blessed are those who are not offended by the cross. Blessed are those who are not offended by the truth in regards to their sin. Blessed are those who endure trage-dies yet continue to trust the Lord. Blessed are those who are not offended by Jesus who says He is the only way to salvation. Blessed are they who have prayed yet haven't seen any change, yet they still rejoice in the Lord. Blessed are those who suffer for their faith and not turn away. Blessed are they who believes, though he tarries, the return of Jesus for those who have given their will and their life to Him. Blessed are those who understand that if we lose our life to Christ, we shall find it again.

5. Be cautious about following the crowd; most times the road going the wrong way is crowded—sounds good, looks good, but at the core will move us so far from God that we, as a whole, will eat from the hand of the enemy. *An apple looks good, but watch out for the worm.* A lie is always set up by some truth; it is a hook in one's jaw that pulls a deceived mind into the boat and bondage of one's own destruction. Feeding on lies always lead to deception and confusion. Sin promises pleasure, yet when it is full grown, it will require our lives and souls. Speeches are prepared to be as sweet as honey; yet over time, sooner than later, it will rot the

teeth of those who have itchy ears (tell me what I want to hear). Once the disease of perversion sets in, the heart of what one was falsely led to believe will begin to uncover their failures and shame. If we shall decide to go our own way (adopt abominations) and lose our fear of God, that which covers us with safety and blessings shall eventually be removed. Turn not to the left nor to the right, but let the Word of God be your standard and truth. Our hope is not in this government, but in His (Jesus) government in our lives. We, who believe, should look up for our salvation draws near!

6. We live in days where people hate the truth and are angered at correction. They rejoice in that which is killing them.

7. Many may not like what I'm about to say, but there is a movement that is destroying our nation from within. This movement seeks to destroy the family unit which is the foundation of our society. This may sound as though women are solely to blame, but it is men who have been given the responsibility to protect the family. This is a shadow of the garden of Eden all over again.

   Some women are so occupied with being equal to men that they are willing to sacrifice their children (both in the womb or out) and even an institution established by God which is the bedrock of a moral society, marriage, in order to validate themselves. Foolishly, they devalue the very thing that makes them invaluable, the purpose of their existence. These women whose goal it is to replace and castrate men are operating out of the curse of fallen humanity. In the end, there will be no satisfaction in their quest. When they look back, they will see all of their accomplishments, but they will feel the emptiness and regret of unfulfilled purpose. A celebration of barrier-breakers is nothing evil within itself, but if operating out of a wound, a spirit not of God will empower it. This worship of female power and dominance over men is facilitated by a curse, and this same spirit is behind the betrayal of all—when a mother kills her own child. Oh, that she may ascend above the glass ceiling of men and, in her eyes, take her rightful place by any means necessary. Not only has she sacrificed her children, but she has sacrificed her role in holding society together by holding the family together. She has sacrificed the soul of our nation, a nation that pushes an agenda to emasculate men and encourage women to leave behind traditional roles for feministic roles. A nation with an agenda to push for the elimination of gender roles and embrace the sick fantasies of being whatever one feels like that day. In the lust for power and dominance, many have once again been deceived by the serpent. Where are the fathers as the blood of her children drips from her hand! Her only salvation is to cover herself and repent.

8. The space between light and distance is time.

9. The end result, preceded by a National Day of Prayer, of the Civil War is what held our country together from secession; and again this same fight in our hearts and minds, if not won in the spirit, will tear this country apart.

10. A snake has a split tongue, and that which is evil is always concealed in good. Honey dipped in poison is still deadly. Don't be fooled by those that speak of God but deny Him in their actions. As a tree, we all are known by the fruit we bear. The soul of this nation will be troubled when we move foundations on which everything we hold dear stands. When we reject the principles of God, we attract deception; and when deception has had her way, a downfall is always soon to follow. Pray for (not against) the hearts of our leaders, and pray for the mercy of God over this nation.

11. This is a warning against the deception of the media and the powers behind it. Please understand I'm not totally against the media; it has its purpose. I am opposed to how some outlets use the airway to push agendas that are destructive to individuals, groups, and this country. I am opposed to the bold divisiveness used to tear each other down in front of God and the world. Where are the examples to our chil-

dren? These seeds of hate planted will someday bear unsavory fruit. Always remember that the Word of God is as an anchor (the only anchor) that keeps us from drifting away from Him.

12. A watchman asleep leaves his people defenseless; but a people asleep, who hears but ignores the warning, will leave themselves in total and complete ruins.

13. We are a walking billboard; we market ourselves by how we carry and conduct ourselves. Every time we keep our word, we tell everyone that we can be trusted. Every time we show up on time; we tell everyone that we are dependable. Every time we do what we're supposed to do without someone having to manage us, we tell everyone that we are committed. Every time we say good things to others about something we are a part of, we show everyone our level of loyalty. Every time we conduct ourselves the same at all times, we show everyone our character. Every time we help someone in need, we show our ability to have compassion. Every time we keep calm in stressful situations, we show our ability to lead. Every time we can forgive and love even our enemies, we are telling everyone that we love God. We don't have to say a word; our actions say it all. So just what are we telling people about us?

14. Don't be so surprised by the world; the world is going to do what the world is going to do. Focus on the area of influence we have to advance the kingdom of God daily. If all of us who believe do this, we will have a huge impact on the world. Dark places will be exposed to the light, and the truth will replace the lie. This is our call! If we are not doing the work of the Lord, what in the world are we doing here?

15. First comes the invasion of privacy and then comes the seizure of freedom.

16. Why is society so obsessed with masculinizing women and feminizing men? Each gender has a role it must play given by the creator. When played the way intended, there is order. We should not let hurt drive us to extremes. If this contin-

ues, the next generation will be so confused that darkness to them will appear to be light, wrong will become right, and lies will be accepted as their truth. If we want to keep the train on the track and not derail a generation, the Word of God should be our only standard of how we should live our lives and not the popular opinion of the perverse culture we live in. The Word of God is not out of date, and it shall never be out of style. Jesus is the truth and the life; anything else is a lie and shall lead to death. We shouldn't cave in to the demands of this Antichrist spirit that is perverting or altogether invalidating the Word of God. Truth is a rock we can build on because it never changes like the shifting sands of the ideologies that are pervasive in our society today. If we have to prove what we are, then maybe that's a sign that we are not so sure ourselves. There is no such thing as your truth; there is only His truth. In order to know what something is and how it works, we have to go back to the manual (the Bible) and discover what the creator intended. The further one gets from that, the more dysfunctional his or her life will be.

If we put a dog in a suit, he will still bark and probably chase cars. If we put a pretty dress on a pig, she will still find a way to wallow. If we throw a cat in the air, more than likely, he will land on his feet. If a woman cuts her hair and, with the help of testosterones, deepens her voice and grows a beard, she is still a woman, maybe an ugly one but a woman. If a man puts on a tutu and runs around with what seems to be a broken wrist, biologically, he is still a male, not a man, an ugly one I might add. To pretend to be something we weren't created to be makes us look silly. We can't change God's design and purpose for every living thing. #itiswhatitis #nothatejusttruth

17. People question whether or not God (Yahweh) is truly loving and merciful. They recite a story about a man who saw the ark of the Covenant falling. He tried to steady it and was struck dead. People, we need to understand that God is

a Holy God. If we touch anything that's his and there is sin in our lives, the penalty of sin has no choice but to visit us. There is no compromise in holiness, and those of us who are playing with God are playing a dangerous game that will soon end not in our favor.

18. Give a fool a platform, and they will act the part. Fear immobilizes us, and anger blinds us.

19. Sin is still sin contrary to what these new-age preachers and false prophets will tell us. God is not okay with our cursing. God is not okay with our stealing and lying. God is not okay with us leading His sheep away with our fleshly doctrines. God is not okay with our perversions and vain imaginations. God is not okay with us shacking up or test driving the car before we buy it (fornication/sex before marriage). God is not okay with our abominations we try to legislature into the fabric of our society. God is not okay with our alternative lifestyles; God is not okay with our "side pieces" or our disrespect to our vows to Him. God is not okay with us prostituting Him or ourselves. God is not okay with divorce; God is not okay with our so-called right to murder unborn destines (babies). God is not okay with our rebellion against authority. God is not okay with our false religion or our witchcraft. God is not okay with our hatred, divisiveness, and racist ideology. God is not okay with our self-righteous filthy spirits. God is not okay with the abusing of our own bodies by pumping drugs and alcohol in them. God is not okay with our "trying" to mock Him, for God is not mocked. Whatsoever a man sows, he shall reap. God is not okay with our idolatry. He will not have any other gods before Him. Our pledge should be to Him alone and nothing else on earth; those of us who are Christians are in this world and not of it. God is not okay with our clubbing on Saturday and being late for church on Sunday. "Well at least I'm in there." Naw, someone who says this is still out there! If our lifestyle is anything below being righteous in Christ, we shouldn't even think about

touching a platform (calling ourselves ministering, leading worship, or playing an instrument for the Lord). We need to sit ourselves down and get free! *God is still holy, and He has called us unto His holiness.*

Know ye not that the unrighteous shall not inherit the kingdom of God? Be not deceived: neither fornicators, nor idolaters, nor adulterers, nor effeminate (homosexuals), nor abusers of themselves with mankind, Nor thieves, nor covetous, nor drunkards, nor revilers, nor extortioners, shall inherit the kingdom of God. And such were some of you: but ye are washed, but ye are sanctified, but ye are justified in the name of the Lord Jesus, and by the Spirit of our God. (1 Corinthian 6: 9–11)

20. No, none of us is without sin; but just like God, we should not be okay with it. We should be humble and quick to repent. No, none of us are righteous in and of ourselves, but we can walk in righteousness through Christ. We should work our own salvation out with fear and trembling! We serve a holy God! Why isn't God okay with all of this stuff? It is simply because He loves us. Would a loving parent warn their children of things to avoid so that things would go well with them? Yes, how much more will the one who is love (Yahweh) warn us of our own pending destruction?

We can't live our lives in such a way that we forget that the wages of sin is death (eternal separation from God), but the gift of God is eternal life in Christ Jesus our Lord. We can fool others and even convince ourselves that a sinful lifestyle is okay with God. But let us never forget that nothing is hidden from God, and He knows the very motives of our hearts. For example, if my motive for writing this is to beat up on people and not love them with the truth, I will have to give account for this when I stand before God. My point is that no matter how dark the world seems to get, in love, we should let our lights shine. Just as we all get mad when someone comes in our room while we are asleep and flip on the light switch, people will get mad at us because the light (revelation) will expose darkness (void of understanding). We must hold the standard that God has called us to. We must give no ground to the devil in our lives. Fear (respect) and rightly represent who God is to the lost world. We must share the good news! We don't have to fit in (curse or have a beer with them, get a tattoo sleeve, get piercings, or be tolerant of a lifestyle that is contrary to the Word of God) to reach them; the goodness of God is enough, and besides, God has already placed it in their hearts to know that they need Him through the Holy Spirit. We must just water the seed, be real with our love, and live, with the help of the Holy Spirit, what we confess. May God create in us a clean heart and renew in us a right spirit.

21. While voting I observed something; my wife and I were standing while waiting for the poles to open. Other people started to come, and one guy who had seemingly an influential personality said, "Hey, let's all form one line." I have voted at this place so many times, and I knew there were always two lines. The one I started was the one I was supposed to be in (I knew what I knew). A few people listened to this charismatic guy. Three of us did not. Pretty soon more and more people showed up; and yes, you guessed it, instead of thinking for themselves, they got into the long line. One of the workers came out and was shocked at the long line that had formed; she said the people who were supposed to be in this line are going to be mad when they get up here and find out that they were in the wrong line. My point is, following the crowd without the right information leads to deception, wasted time, and disappointment. As some of those voters in the wrong line, some of us will be disappointed when we get up there on judgement day because we will find out that we had been listening to the wrong voice. As my wife and I did this morning, if you

know truth, stand on it even if you have to stand alone. God with us is more than the whole world against us. With Jesus, we are never alone. Wide is the gate that leads to destruction, but narrow is the way that leads to our salvation. When we vote, not so much as who we are voting for, we must know what we are voting for. This is what we will be held accountable for, and claiming ignorance will not be an excuse because we have the Word of God. Selah.

22. It is a lot harder running away from Christ than running to Him. In His arms is where we were meant to be.

23. "And if a stranger sojourn with thee in your land, ye shall not vex him. But the stranger that dwelleth with you shall be unto you as one born among you, and thou shalt love him as thyself; for ye were strangers in the land of Egypt: I am the Lord your God" (Leviticus 19:33–34, KJV)

24. The things that really matter in life can't be bought.

25. We should never get so used to drama that we get bored with normal living.

26. In life, there are principles that, if violated, will not produce that which we hope for. If we want corn from a garden, we must plant corn in the garden. Not only that, when the corn is ready, we must go get it or else what we hoped for will rot before our eyes.

27. The devil doesn't always come through the front door. He's a thief, and he would love nothing more than to steal our time.

28. A news anchor on CNN got mad last night at a lady who represented evangelicals. He argued that the church and its pastors should not be allowed to preach "hate" against gays (he being gay himself) and be allowed to keep their tax-free exemption status. He was furious, and he finally said, "Well we are going to have to agree to disagree." What he doesn't understand is that in the end, our opinions will not be worth a hill of beans. Yes, we have a choice to live our lives however we want (God wants disciples and not robots), but in the end, whether or not we lived the truth

found in the Word of God (not man's opinion) will determine whether or not God will say that he knows us and we belong to him (enter his rest). The spirit (antichrist) that embolden this anchor last night was furious at the church because it seems that the church is the last and only voice telling him and others like him the truth about their lifestyle. It's not hatred; it is truth and love warning him and others like him of the wages of sin which is eternal separation from God and death. If I was headed in the dark off a cliff, I would consider it love if some brave soul warned me about what was up ahead of me. Get ready, church. The next step for gays and lesbians is to silence the church by declaring that our love warning is hate speech.

Leaders get the church finances in order so we will not be hirelings bought and told what to say by a government that is anti-Christ. If leaders allow the truth to be silenced, those leaders will not have a church. Their church will just be a gathering of fools; to fear (respect/reverence) the Lord (not the government/unrighteous laws) is the beginning of wisdom. It's coming, so what will we do? Be ashamed of the gospel or stand for righteousness and truth. The Bible (God's word) should be the final authority that governs our lives.

29. What destroys a man is taking away his pride of being a man, his pride of him being responsible for himself and the ones he loves. Personal responsibility produces a strength and an identity given to a man by God to manage the world He lives in.

30. We should never make politics our religion.

31. Sin has to be confronted and not comforted. And if the confronted run away, they can run, but they can't hide from the truth of love and their need for God. It is when people get uncomfortable that it is even possible for change or repentance to happen in their hearts. *The gospel was never meant to accommodate us, but to change us.*

32. This post is not to be insensitive to the struggles of the poor; I've been there, and I've done that; I didn't like it,

and that is what motivated me to rise above it by the grace of God. Let's talk about the proposed raising of the minimum wage to $15 an hour (almost double the current minimum wage). Will this move erase the middle class? Why do I ask? I'm glad you asked. If McDonald's have to pay all of its workers $15 an hour, it would significantly cut into McDonald's profits. This will result in laying off workers (more unemployment) and cause the cost of a happy meal to make parents unhappy. If wages doubled, it is not inconceivable to believe that the cost to eat at McDonald's will double. This will result in the minimum wage earner to be right back in the struggle they thought the federal government was helping them out of. The new cost of the happy meal will eat away at their newly increased wages. Now, here is the kicker: while the minimum wage earner will not be any better off, the middle-class earner will experience inflation, with no pay increase. Translation: the middle-class earner will be worse off. This equals more people in the struggle to survive at the mercy of the government. Now, this scenario is just at McDonald's; what about the rest of our economy? No, thank you! Somebody, please think before it's too late!

A sensible solution: if you really want to help minimum wage workers, attach an increase in wage to rise at the same time as inflation (smaller increments but in step with living increases). In the meantime, a "small" increase to the minimum wage based on the inflation that hasn't been raised since July 24, 2009. This will help those struggling but will not shock the economy. Also, offer grants for minimum-wage earners who needs and want "help" with more education or skill development so they will be qualified for jobs that pay higher wages. Always remember that poverty is an issue that no amount of money can fix. If it could, it would have been fixed a long time ago. If we are not faithful over little, we will never be ruler over much. Having money is about stewardship!

33. We have no problem with trusting God with our past, but we want to hold on to the future. "Take no thought on tomorrow." In other words, if we are in God, we should not worry. Who do we trust with our future? If it's ourselves or someone else, we are in trouble. God knows the beginning of our life to the end of our lives. I'll take my chances with God. I think of Abraham how God just told him to go without telling him where, and Abraham trusted God. It was count unto him as righteousness. That type of faith will always get us to where we were meant to be. The safest place to be is in the will of God. It matters not how backward our world has turned. We must share our hope and have faith that God has not brought us this far to leave us. *The battle against us is to steal our faith,* so do not let anything or anyone steal our faith that God is who He said he is, and He will do what He said He will do. Hold on to His promises, and remind Him (He didn't forget) of His Word. There are things that must happen in this world so that prophecy can be fulfilled, so think it not strange when you see these things happening. Just know it's a part of the plan, and to us who are in Christ, we shall overcome by the blood of the lamb and the word of his testimony.

34. Being honest about the past helps to heal the future. The past is the wisdom of the present.

35. Make no mistake about it; this is indeed a battle for the very soul of America. Will she be saved, or will she be lost? On a respirator of hope, frail, and in need of healing, in what shape will we leave America to our children? We are not voting about the sins of two men as the media and many others would have us to believe; it's about the sins of a nation and the pending judgement of a people. Will we return to God and humble ourselves before Him, or will we, in our pride, go our own way and continue down a path of perversion and the innocent blood shed of millions? The vote will not be about our offenses, parties, opinions, or preferences; it will simply be a vote for life or for death for

America and our children. Choose life, give our children a chance, and leave the rest to God!

36. Our praise is a weapon against sorrow.

37. To lose the fear of God is to be already dead and not know it yet.

38. Faith—the only thing by which we are saved. There is a fight in this present atmosphere to erase God from our society, and the only way to do that is to steal the faith of those whom put their trust in God. For it is those who believe that light the way (through their faith) for those who have yet to believe. In the storms of life, faith, as a lighthouse, guides us safely ashore. Those without faith endure the crashing waves of life with no direction or assurance of their salvation. In the tempest we call life, they sail in the darkness of deception headed full speed to destruction. They live in hell with only the promise of death and more hell in the here and after. If only they had a light house to show them the way to the kingdom, some would remain blind and go full speed ahead while others would open their eyes and be drawn to the light. We, who believe, must keep the faith and not be offended of God in spite of our trials and persecution; we must shine the light within us (the hope of salvation) for those who have yet to see. We are the light of the world; may Jesus find faith and oil in our lamps upon his return!

39. If the only thing we can do for a person is give them hope, then we have done more than enough.

40. Don't let fear set up camp where faith used to be in your life!

41. Everything in this life will change except God. He is like the North Star we can look up to gauge where we are. He is the one constant in this life.

42. What we see is not conclusive evidence of the state of our situation. Behind the scenes of life there is a greater thing at work. Not seeing change doesn't mean that things are not changing.

43. Positions remain, but the people in those positions come and go. We should never dishonor a position even if we don't like the person in the position. To dishonor the position is to destroy the power and the authority of that position. What have we done to the power and authority of the position of the president of United States? Better yet, what have we done with the power and authority of the position of God of heaven and earth in our lives?

44. Although this message is focused in one area, it is not bias in that it ignores a common problem we all have, and that is sin. It's easy to point out this particular sin, but we should all examine our own hearts for hidden sin. It is important to be mindful of the fact that God will someday soon judge it all. This message is just about this particular sin (which is a sin against our own bodies) and a call for us as a society and a people to turn away from things that separates us from God before it's permanent (the day of judgement). It is not intended to hurt but to heal with the truth. Love is confrontational in that it will stand between us and hell. There is a falling away of marriage, of manhood, and of womanhood. Women want to be men; men want to be woman, and many are refusing to marry. It is a state of confusion. If we are awake and paying close attention, we will notice an uptick of the display of alternative lifestyles in commercials, movies, and even now public libraries and school curriculums. We are witnessing the normalization and indoctrination of something God, our creator, has deemed forbidden, but we the created thing, in defiance, audaciously presume to know better than the one who formed us from the dust of the ground and breathe life into our lungs.

We have redefined love as tolerance when, in fact, anything tolerated outside of the will of God is the opposite of love. It is the eating of the forbidden fruit all over again. Why do we think a loving Father would tell us not to do something? Parents want to see their children succeed financially, spiritually, socially, and emotionally; but more importantly, they want to keep them safe from things that could be harmful and literally hazardous to their health.

This agenda that is being pushed so hard, is rooted in rebellion against the creator, the one who knows how we should function based on His design. This "lost" cause comes with a curse. To support this agenda, we either don't believe God (Yahweh) is the creator; or we just willfully, out of loving fleshy pleasure more than God, align ourselves with this anti-Christ spirit. There is no mixing of the two; we either love one, or we hate the other. God will never change His mind on this because it goes against his nature. It perverts what he created, and it has no viable way of being fruitful or multiplying. It flat-out goes against creation.

God created a man and a woman for a reason; their design complimented each other, and they were a perfect fit. Their union, by design, could be fruitful and multiple. My point: what will be the consequences of our continued push to rebel against God on this issue? The devil's dream is a godless society, but unfortunately for him, there will always be a remnant. The consequence of our society's rebellion, after many warnings, is judgement. The Holy Father will judge sin, and His will shall be done on earth as it is in heaven. It may seem like darkness is winning, but it is just a loving Father being patient by giving us time to return to Him. There will be a day when that time will run out, and I truly believe that's soon. Don't let Satan come between what God has joined and ordained. *Always remember this one thing that love is confrontational in that it will stand between us and hell.*

CHAPTER 7

The Season of Reckoning:
An End in Sight

> But and if that evil servant shall say in his heart, My lord delayeth his coming; and shall begin to smite his fellowservants, and to eat and drink with the drunken; the lord of that servant shall come in a day when he looketh not for him, and in an hour that he is not aware of, and shall cut him asunder, and appoint him his portion with the hypocrites: there shall be weeping and gnashing of teeth. (Matthew 24:48–51)

ONCE UPON A TIME, LIFE began; and just like it began, it shall end. The last chapter of the story of life will end in a dramatic fashion according to Bible prophecy which are words given to us from men inspired by the Spirit of God. According to biblical prophecy, conditions on the earth will continue to deteriorate until Christ returns. The beginning of the end has started and the nations of this world are beginning to reap the harvest of the seeds of their disobedience and defiance toward God (Yahweh). Lawlessness and violence are escalating and more so as the day approaches. At some point, right before the rapture of the church (true surrendered believers to Christ), nations will be against nations and kingdoms will be against kingdoms. The threat of conventional, biological, chemical, electronic, cyber, nuclear, and possibly even space (Star Wars) warfare will be an unsettling reality many will face.

As the result of man's unwillingness to repent, the curse of drought and famine shall touch close to everyone's home. Locusts, wildfires, and the lack of rain will lead to food shortage in places unexpected. The heavens will shut up and the effects of famine will be felt by everyone. Whoever owns the most farmland will control the world through their bellies. Is this why Bill Gates is now the largest farmland owner with 242,000 acres? Is this why a Chinese company now owns 146,000 acres of prime US farmland? The big players in the end are setting the stage.

With an already soaring national debt in almost every country of the world, there will be inflation such as this generation has never seen. As America and the nations of this world defy God in their perversions, nature will turn on us and not be so motherly. The earth will experience frequent earthquakes (contractions of something coming) in places unexpected and natural catastrophes on scales of biblical proportions according to Matthew 24:7. We have already experienced one of the greatest public health crises in a century. Now, around the world, many public health officials and ministers are raising concerns about diseases, viruses, pestilences, plagues, and deadly contagious pandemics. Our latest pandemic health crisis has revealed just how vulnerable we are in managing health crisis such as these. The latest pandemic has crippled economies, breached hospital capacities, and has killed over 500,000 people, in the US as of February 22, 2021, especially the most vulnerable among us.

There are events currently happening that raise awareness of the biblical account of the end and the return of Jesus Christ:

-   the rise in Islamic extremist
-   the rise of the European Union's influence
-   the rise of false religious leaders and false teachings
-   the rise in Christian persecution
-   the rise of anti-Semitism, a world focused on Israel, and the number of Jews returning home
-   the rise of violence and murder (hearts waxing cold)
-   technology ability to spread the gospel to all nations of the earth

- talks about the rebuilding of the third temple in Jerusalem and a school training priests on temple rituals
- the establishment of the US embassy in Jerusalem
- traditional morals becoming less accepted
- gender wars and the gay and lesbian agenda being indoctrinated in the next generations through curriculums and media; and an American President granting a blanket authorization to fly pride flags at embassies around the world
- the continued slaughter of the unborn (abortions)
- rising tensions with the threat of wars worldwide—food shortages, water shortages, droughts, asteroid threats, extreme weather patterns, the beginning signs of inflations, mounting debt, and earthquakes and volcanoes eruptions in unusual places.
- Israel signing a peace agreement with the United Arab Emirates
- Economic turmoil and a bubble of national debt that is unsustainable in America and most nations of the world (America is projected to soar above 30 trillion in 2021)
- the level of mistrust in the media and the level of fear and distrust in government, religious, and CDC leaders
- the rise in gene editing (CRISPR); China is playing god by using this technology to experiment on humans to genetically engineer biologically enhanced soldiers according to an article by Nolan Peterson. This could be a sign that war is coming. The age of genetic superiority has begun.

Deception and the False Church

This know also, that in the last days perilous times shall come. For men shall be lovers of their own selves, covetous, boasters, proud, blasphemers, disobedient to parents, unthankful, unholy, Without natural affection, trucebreakers, false accusers, incontinent, fierce, despisers of those that are good, Traitors, heady, highminded, lovers of pleasures more than lovers of God; Having a form of godliness, but denying the power thereof: from such turn away. For of this sort are they which creep into houses, and lead captive silly women laden with sins, led away with divers lusts, Ever learning, and never able to come to the knowledge of the truth. (2 Timothy 3:1–7, KJV)

Today, the atmosphere is crowded with lies and liars. It's hard to navigate through the deception to get to the truth. Who can you trust? What can you trust? Who do you believe? Who will deceive? What is the truth? Where is the proof? There have been so many lies told that it's difficult to know who or what to trust or who to believe. Deception is and will be Satan's weapon against humanity in the last days—the days in which we live. Deception now floods the airways of our society and even in some pulpits. Everyone has an opinion, and to them, it's all that matters. Where is the fear of the Lord? Think it not strange when we wake up in an environment that embraces the snares of lies. An environment where brother will betray brother to death and a father his child. An environment where children will rebel against their parents and have them put to death. The alarms are going off, yet many who have ears refuse to hear or search out the biblical explanation of where time is taking us. We live in a time where people despise the truth because their hearts are set on their own affections and lusts. They are neither convicted or convinced of their folly. Their hearts have hardened against God, and an anti-Christ spirit has taken control of their actions and agendas. The stage is being set; nations are taking their positions. Little by little, Satan is conditioning and preparing the world for His greatest deception—to declare himself the savior of the world.

There is a false church that once was a bearer of the light; but false doctrine, religion, and the traditions of men has caused the Word of God to be of no affect to convict of sin nor to hear the voice of the one true living God. Humanism and secret sins have eroded trust and has shaken the faith of the once faithful.

Beware of the false prophet; he speaks with the snake's tongue. He claims to represent God on earth, but his heart is revealed through his words, which are not words from God. He will lead many away from truth by their own desires and marry them to the sweet lies of his deception. They will fall in strange beds because they listen to and trust perverse lips. He claims righteousness while supporting and now openly promoting blasphemies and abominations. He tries to take Christ and unify Him with a harlot. He persecutes those in his own order, and the image he has sold has been brought by the gullible. In the basket of faith, his apple has caused a rot; and as a spot, his dogma spreads because his title is influential and infectious. He, himself, has become an abomination ready to serve and fulfill the desolation of all things holy. His teachings are increasingly against Christ, and his loyalty has shifted with the wind. He has a huge following that refuse to question or challenge him because His image to them is holy and infallible. His flag is up, and many have pledged their unwavering allegiance. The course has been set, and they will be destroyed because of their lack of knowledge. He will endorse peace through one-world religion and safety through a one-world solution. It all sounds so great, but it is diabolical in nature. Our only defense against the illusion (image, deception) is to stand on the infallible Word of God! Beware of the serpent's tongue! Know what God said (we must read our Bible), know the truth, and don't deviate from it. Those that sleep, sleep at night, but those who are awake can see the light (truth).

> And he said to them all, If any man will come after me, let him deny himself, and take up his cross daily, and follow me. For whosoever will save his life shall lose it: but whosoever will lose his life for my sake, the same shall save it. (Luke 9:23–24)

Since the beginning of our existence, Satan has encouraged our rebellion to God by saying, "You shall not surely die." He has encouraged us through the deception that we can do what we want to do, live however we want to live, say whatever we want to say, marry whomever or whatever we want to marry, worship whomever or whatever we want to worship, and do with our bodies whatever and with whomever we want to do it with. He deceives us with a little truth mixed with his lies. Yes, God is a God of love, but He is also holy and a God of justice and wrath. What He says is exactly what He means. The wages of sin (transgression against God's divine law) is death. What we think about it, feel about it, and what Satan says about it does not change what the law requires for sin which is blood. This is justice, and yes, also God is a God of mercy. He gave the blood of His Son (Jesus) to take the place of the blood that is required of us all. He is the supreme judge; no one selected Him or confirmed Him. Someday soon, we all will have to stand before Him and give an account for every word, act, or deed done upon the earth. It will be very wise of us to retain Jesus as our attorney. It will cost us nothing except our full commitment to Him alone. When offenses are read before all in the court of heaven, there will be no justification for our deeds. "I didn't know. I've been hurt by the church. I was molested as a child. I was raped by someone I trusted. I was poor, I never felt loved. I was a mistake, or Satan tricked me" will not be enough of a defense to set us free. Even when Mother Theresa's verdict was read, it came back guilty. God, whom is just in all His ways, will have no choice but to say, "Depart from me you worker of iniquity; I never knew you." It won't matter that we were a pastor, president, or priest. If we didn't work our salvation out with fear and trembling on earth by accepting His son, we must leave His holy presence. But wait! If Jesus is our attorney, He will stand up for us and show the supreme judge and all of creation the blood that was shed for our full pardon! That's justice and mercy working together! Praise God!

Are we in last days of the church? What will the condition of the church be right before the return of Jesus? Is the last church mention in Revelation 3:14–23, a mirror of the state of the church today?

And unto the angel of the church of the Laodiceans write; These things saith the Amen, the faithful and true witness, the beginning of the creation of God; I know thy works, that thou art neither cold nor hot: I would thou wert cold or hot. So then because thou art lukewarm, and neither cold nor hot, I will spue thee out of my mouth. Because thou sayest, I am rich, and increased with goods, and have need of nothing; and knowest not that thou art wretched, and miserable, and poor, and blind, and naked: I counsel thee to buy of me gold tried in the fire, that thou mayest be rich; and white raiment, that thou mayest be clothed, and that the shame of thy nakedness do not appear; and anoint thine eyes with eyesalve, that thou mayest see. As many as I love, I rebuke and chasten: be zealous therefore, and repent. Behold, I stand at the door, and knock: if any man hears my voice, and open the door, I will come in to him, and will sup with him, and he with me. To him that overcometh will I grant to sit with me in my throne, even as I also overcame, and am set down with my Father in his throne. He that hath an ear, let him hear what the Spirit saith unto the churches. (Revelation 3:14–22)

If we lose focus of our first love and be lured asleep by the lust, deception, and perversion of this present world, we will deny the faith. According to Matthew 5:13–14, "We are the salt of the Earth, but what good is salt if it loses it favor." We are the light of the world, but what good is the light if no one can see it? What good are we if no one sees Jesus in us because maybe He is no longer in us? We either love one or we hate the other, and if we don't choose Christ, we automatically chose the other. If we claim to be the bride of Christ, every moment of our lives should be about preparing for His return that will be when we least expect Him. The taking away of the believers is what is referred to as the Rapture. Many say that this is made up because it is not mention in the old testament. The reason the Rapture was not mention in the old testament is because the gentiles (us or non-Jews) had not been grafted in yet. That didn't happen until the New Testament. It was concealed unto the appointed time. Timing is everything; we must all repent while there is still time so that we don't miss our own wedding!

Time to Go Home

> Remember therefore how thou hast received and heard, and hold fast, and repent. If therefore thou shalt not watch, I will come on thee as a thief, and thou shalt not know what hour I will come upon thee. (Revelation 3:3)

Growing up when the streetlights came on as darkness started to move in, we knew that it was time to go home. It was a sign to us that the day has ended, and that there was only a little time left to make it home before the wrath of our mothers were pour out on us. At the end of the day, there is always an accounting of something; biblically we call it judgement day, a day when all of our works on the earth will be weighed, and we will either be found guilty or innocent. The reality of the whole thing is that none of us are innocent; we all are guilty of transgressing God's laws. We are all guilty of sin in which we all, by law, must pay for. There is one problem; the cost is too high for us to pay because it would cost us eternal death or separation from our creator, God (Yahweh). In His justice, God has declared that "vengeance is mine; I will repay saith the Lord." This is God's day of reckoning. God is a God of justice, and he must settle the accounts of every man. As implied in Galatians 6:7, books are being kept: "Be not deceived; God is not mocked: for whatsoever a man soweth, that shall he also reap," and according to Matthew 12:36, nothing will be left out. "But I say unto you, that every idle word that men shall speak, they shall give account thereof in the day of judgement."

We all will be found guilty and will not have a defense to justify our deeds except for this one thing. Our God is a God of wrath and justice, but He is as equally merciful. He has given us a way of escape from the penalty we deserve, and that's through the best defense attorney a repentant heart can secure—Jesus Christ. He is the high priest that can be touched with the feeling of our infirmities. In other words, because of His experience on earth, He can relate to us. He was in all points tempted like us, yet He was without sin. He is the only perfect sacrifice that qualifies as payment for all of our sins. The only thing we have to do is accept Him, through faith, what He did for us on the cross by shedding His innocent blood for the remission of our sins. If we do so, on that day, when we have to stand before the judge of the universe and the verdict comes back guilty, Jesus will stand with us and say, "Look, Father, it's paid in full." Then our Holy God will not see us in the state we are in, but He will see Himself in us through the blood of His son that covers us. Our guilty verdict will be overturned, and we shall enter His rest.

While on earth "with the streetlights not yet on," we should labor or work to enter his rest lest we are lured to unbelief. We should always discern the times, and be ready to go home in a moment's notice. We should fight against the temptation that there is plenty of time to get things right with the Lord. We should fight against the apathy that sneaks in to replace our passion for the things of God. Being an American or going to church doesn't make us a Christian, nor does being a good person saves our soul. If we have not truly accepted Jesus and what He did on the cross for us, NOW is the time for time is short. We must seek Him while he may be found. It matters not what we have done; it matters what we do now! We must put our faith and trust in Jesus, ask for forgiveness, surrender, and accept Him as the Lord of our lives which means everything we do is about Him. By losing our lives to Him on earth, He will save our lives from death for all of eternity!

> Behold, I shew you a mystery; We shall not all sleep, but we shall all be changed, in a moment, in the twinkling of an eye, at the last trump: for the trumpet shall sound, and the dead shall be raised incorruptible, and we shall be changed. (1 Corinthians 15:51–52)

If we knew about the time, day, or hour a burglar was coming to our house, we would wait for him. It is the unexpected times that the thief comes, and it would be wise for us to always be ready lest sudden destruction befalls our home. The same is true in relation to our knowledge of when Jesus will return, but it is given to us that it will be a time that we least expect it. Just as that unsuspecting thief or a Jewish bride, we should always be ready with no notice. Once Jesus returns, it will be too late to get oil for our lamps. Just like in the days of Noah, at the first drop of rain, the door to our salvation will be closed. Woe to those who are caught faithless, unknown by God, deceived, unfaithful, in rebellion, unrepentant, unprepared, in idolatry, in abominations and lasciviousness, and without love in their hearts. Woe to the self-righteous and blasphemers. Look up! The smell of rain is our warning, and the darkness of empty lamps is our sign. We don't have to be perfect to go in the Rapture. We just have to belong to Jesus.

In the end-times, according to biblical prophecy, the world will turn their focus to the center of the earth and the apple of God's eye, the land of Israel. America and Israel have always been friends and allies deeply rooted together because of shared values. In America's constitution, the influence of Jewish tradition is evident on America's founding fathers. America's government was modeled after the Hebrew Commonwealth. The deep ties between America and Israel seem to be a spiritual bond as well, for we can't even spell the capital of Israel JerUSAsalm (first recognized by the United States president Donald Trump on December 6, 2017, but rejected by the United Nation Security Council) without seeing the USA in the center. So if the nations of the world in Bible prophesy come to do battle and destroy Israel, where is America? Where is America in Bible prophecy? Written before the birth of America, we can find her in Ezekiel 38. "Sheba, and Dedan, and the merchants of Tarshish, with *all the young lions* thereof, shall say unto thee, Art thou come to take a spoil? hast thou gathered thy company to take a prey? to carry away silver and gold, to take away cattle and goods, to take a great spoil" (Ezekiel 38:13). We see Ethiopia (Sheba), Saudi Arabia (Dedan), England (merchants of Tarshish), and all of young lions in this passage of scripture. It is believed by many Bible scholars that the young lions in Ezekiel 38 represents the future superpower, America.

Why isn't America on the main stage during the end-times? Why doesn't America play a more dominant role in end-times world events? Is it because her sins have become so great against God that she is diminished from inside out, or could it be that America is diminished because of the number of people taken in the Rapture? We know that it will be like the days of Noah where people will be married and given in marriage according to Jesus; that doesn't sound like an America or any country being totally destroyed. The Rapture or the disappearing of millions of people in America will cause mass devastation because systems and government will have few people to run them at first. Once the Rapture or taking away of the saints takes place, then comes seven years of great tribulation which include massive deaths and destruction.

Out of chaos, the anti-Christ will declare himself the savior of the world. He will declare peace and safety, something the world will long for. Then once the lie he perpetrates is accepted, there will be sudden destruction upon the earth. There will be no escape from the things that will befall the earth; by then it will be too late.

> For God hath not appointed us to wrath, but to obtain salvation by our Lord Jesus Christ, Who died for us, that, whether we wake or sleep, we should live together with him. (1 Thessalonians 5:9–10)

The Rapture is not a fairytale or a theology of escapism, and no, the word *rapture* does not appear in the text of the Bible because of how it is translated; the word is a description of how we will be taken away or caught up to meet the Lord. According to research done by David Hebert 2006 on the Rapture of the church, *rapture* comes from the Latin word *rapere*, meaning rapid, and the Latin word *rapiemur*, meaning "we shall be caught up." This word was taken from the Greek verb *harpazo*, meaning "to seize upon, spoil, snatch away or take to oneself." *Harpazo* is translated "caught up or "caught away" the five times (out of thirteen) it appears in the Bible relating to Rapture. The other eight times it is translated, "to forcibly seize upon, snatch away, take to oneself or use force on someone." The bottom line is that the Rapture describes how we will be taken away which will be almost unmeasurable speed. It will be a sudden event that will shock the world because some will be taken, and some (those who refused Jesus) will be left behind to endure the great tribulation and the wrath of God.

> For I know the thoughts that I think toward you, saith the Lord, thoughts of peace, and not of evil, to give you an expected end. (Jeremiah 29:11)

Throughout the Bible, we have pictures of God saving his people from His wrath such as Noah and Lot.

> And as it was in the days of Noe, so shall it be also in the days of the Son of man. They did eat, they drank, they married wives, they were given in marriage, until the day that Noah entered into the ark, and the flood came, and destroyed them all. Likewise, also as it was in the days of Lot; they did eat, they drank, they bought, they sold, they planted, they builded; But the same day that Lot went out of Sodom it rained fire and brimstone from heaven, and destroyed them all. Even thus shall it be in the day when the Son of man is revealed. (Luke 17:26–30)

Last but not least, Jesus saved us from the death we deserved.

> For they themselves report concerning us the kind of reception we had among you, and how you turned to God from idols to serve the living and true God, and to wait for his Son

> from heaven, whom he raised from the dead,
> Jesus who delivers us from the wrath to come. (1
> Thessalonians 1:9–10)

History is a witness to God's intention on saving those who believe and love Him from the wrath of Tribulation. Do we dare say or believe that Jesus would abuse His bride before He takes her to His Father's house? As she, the bride, waits, she gets herself ready. Jesus said, "Watch ye therefore, and pray always, that ye may be accounted worthy to escape all these things that shall come to pass, and to stand before the Son of man" (Luke 21:36).

> Because thou hast kept the word of my
> patience, I also will keep thee from the hour of
> temptation, which shall come upon all the world,
> to try them that dwell upon the earth. (Revelation
> 3:10)

Before us all is either life or death. We can use our will to live however we want to live for seventy to eighty years, or we can live according to God's will and live forever. This is the choice that is before us. The dead and the living that belong to Christ shall be raptured up or meet the Lord in the air at the sound of a trumpet's blast, but those who do not belong to Christ will remain on earth and have to go through the tribulation or the wrath of God on those who rejected Him.

A Message to those left Behind

The following message was written by Mark Correll. He gave this information to us to leave behind for our loved ones who may be left behind once Jesus raptures (return for and take away) His church (those who have accepted his bride price and are married to him). Consider yourself my loved one because Jesus loves you.

If you are reading this after the unexplained disappearing of millions of people, this message is for you. If the Rapture has already taken place and you are reading this, take heed to what I'm about to say. The rapture has left a void because Millions of people have suddenly vanished. Economies will collapse overnight, and fear will cause many hearts to fail. There is still hope, but it will be hard, to say the least. You will still have a chance, but you will literally have to go through hell to make it to heaven. You probably will not physically survive, and more than likely you will suffer tremendously. Right now, your soul is what is important because the suffering on earth does not even register in comparison to the suffering of a lost soul in eternity. You will need to survive for seven years in order for this great tribulation to pass. Survival is possible, but it will be rare. There may be massive global earthquakes happening at the same time. Volcano will erupt all over the world, and huge tidal waves will drown many up to more than 20,000 people at a time. There will be such destruction. Famine will be everywhere, and you will probably have to die for your faith.

1. Do not believe the explanation the media give you about the disappearing of millions of people. They will lie and tell you that it is because of alien evaders or some weird virus. Do not believe them.
2. Get rid of your cell phone or any other technical device. They will use them to track you down and kill you. Go off the grid.
3. Do not kill yourself, but pray for the help of the Holy Spirit. The Holy Spirit can still help you even though it was taken out of the world with the rapture of the church. He

can come on individuals like He did in the old testament. There is still hope.

4. Repent immediately; Ask God to forgive you and to come into your heart. If you call on the name of the Lord, He will hear you. This is your last chance.

5. Find a hard copy bible; again, technology will be used as a tracking device. God's word shall never pass away; He will speak to you through His Word. Read the Ten commandments in Exodus Chapter 20. You will be tempted to steal, kill, and use drugs to the numb the pain of your suffering. If you commit these sins, you will find it very difficult to repent.

6. Do not listen to past sermons about future prophecy. Don't listen to what men think will happen. Study Daniel chapter 2 and 7 and all of Revelation. Because you are living in it every day, you will understand it better than anyone ever have.

7. Get off the grid and leave everything except survival supplies behind. Your possessions will not do you any good in the tribulation. Get out of the city and learn to live off the land. Stock up on food supplies and find you a place near running water. Don't forget first aid supplies.

8. Do not go to church; stay away from people as much as possible. "Christian" churches will still be open, and there will still be "Christian" pastors behind pulpits. They will be state and government run churches. They are traps for anyone who genuinely want to be saved because these churches are aligning themselves with the anti-Christ. They will have lying wonders and signs everywhere. It's a deception. The false prophet will control all religions, and all the Godly ministers were taken in the rapture. Just read your bible.

9. Look for hidden signs from fellow believers. They are the only ones you can trust now even above family and "Friends." Help each other.

10. Expect and pray for miracles. You can expect help from God to meet your needs because you will be totally dependent on God.

11. Pray for strength. It will be almost impossible to survive, but the Lord will hear your request. You will need His strength and not your own.

12. Refuse any and all government handouts. With the disappearance of so many, there will be a redistribution of the wealth, but there will be a cost, more than likely your soul.

13. Do not take any marks in your body to buy and sell. If you do, you will belong to Satan forever. It will be better for you to lose your life on Earth than to be damned with Satan in the lake of fire forever.

14. Never deny Jesus; If we deny him, he will deny us. That is game over.

15. Be prepared to suffer; camps of torture will be operating around the clock.

16. If you don't survive, you will gain a crown as a tribulation martyr; your place will be under the alter of God. It will be such a great honor. You will be so close to God.

17. Be determined to endure until the end; there is still hope. Place your hope in the Lord.

18. Remember in spite of being left, God loves you. Suffering may endure for the night but joy shall come in the morning.

> Let us hear the conclusion of the whole matter: Fear God, and keep his commandments: for this is the whole duty of man. For God shall bring every work into judgment, with every secret thing, whether it be good, or whether it be evil. (Ecclesiastes 12:13–14)

Selah 7:1–44

1. Just as in the days of Noah, people mocked him and probably called him an idiot for building a massive boat on dry

ground. He told them that it was going to rain, not fully understanding what rain was, but he believed the words of God, just as some of us are being mocked and being called an idiot for believing something that we have never seen before. We must keep sharing the truth to the lost. We must keep building that bridge between lost humanity and God. We must point the way for them, for if God said it's going to rain, we would be wise to cover our heads for it shall rain. If Jesus said he shall come back for us (His bride), we should keep the light on because He is coming. So let them laugh and mock, but never stop reaching out for them. That's true love!

2. I woke up early this morning after dreaming about people that I know that need to hear this. I clearly saw their faces. I had a sense of urgency because time is short. I'm not writing this to judge anyone; if anything, it's a judgement on me for seeing their lifestyles and not speaking up out of love sooner because of fear of being called judgmental (if you are guilty of this, raise your hand). God is the righteous judge who sits high and looks low. He knows the very motive and intent of every heart, including my own. Nothing is hidden from Him. If this makes us uncomfortable, let us allow the Holy Spirit to convict us, and then there will be no need to worry about being judged.

Out of the abundance of the heart, the mouth speaks. You can tell what's in a person heart by what they say. If there is a curse there, all you will hear coming from them are curses. If there is love, you will hear and feel the love in their words. If there is bitterness, their words will leave a bad taste for us to chew on. If there is faith, their words will leave us uplifted and inspired to trust God. I guess you get my point; whatever is going on inside us will show up outside of us. *Our speech betrays us every time we open our mouths because it reveals the secrets of our hearts.* If we listen closely to ourselves and others, we will know everything we need to know. We have got to keep our hearts right with

God. The heart is exceedingly wicked; who can know and trust the heart? This is why we should daily be on our faces before God saying, "Lord search my heart; create in me a right spirit and a clean heart."

Some of us go to church and think that's supposed to make us okay with God. We have one foot in the church every time the doors are open and one foot in the world when the bars or gossip lines are open. Our speech and actions look no different than that of the world. Some of us do good things and feel as though we are good people. We think that's supposed to make us okay with God. Our "goodness" or righteousness is as filthy rags (worthless) when it comes to being okay (reconciled) to God. The only thing that will ever make us okay with God is faith and the acceptance of His Son for the remission of our sins. Faith and the blood of Jesus applied to our lives transforms us. With the help of the Holy Spirit, we begin to sound like, walk like, love like, and forgive like Jesus. It's no longer a fleshly act, but it becomes a lifestyle with or without an audience. It becomes grievous to us to sin or do sinful things. Goodness, love, and mercy becomes supernaturally natural.

Seriously, folks, do we not know that our lives could be required of us this day. It's time out for religious games and exercises. Don't get left behind saying, "But Lord, I preached in your name, taught Sunday school, served on the usher board, sang on the praise team, did outreach, and was faithful to church" (He wants you to be faithful to Him) only to hear, "Depart from me you worker of iniquity; I never knew you!" It's a terrible thing to know the truth and not truly live it in your heart. We may know of God, but does He know us? Are our names written in the Lamb's Book of Life? Have we been intimate (one with, close, truly connected) with the Lord? Have we gone to the secret place (spend time) with Him? Have we surrendered every area (finances, relationships, etc.) of our lives to Him? Time is short! God is not mocked; whatsoever we sow, that also shall we reap. The need for salvation is ever so clear these days surrounded by so much fear and death (you don't have to be old to die these days). It's time we all took a knee (in submission to God) to examine our own hearts and lives. Lord, help me to be found faithful!

3. When judgement comes, it comes for everyone, but the only saving grace for some is the blood of a lamb that takes their place.

4. Truth is like a bitter pill; it's tough to swallow, but if we can just get it in us, it will heal everything that ails us.

5. How is it that billions of people believe in other planets, the solar system, the universe, and galaxies, all of which are things 99.9 percent of them haven't seen for themselves? How is it that billions of people believe in these things based off of pictures without question, but not believe the creator, God, of the Holy Bible, Yahweh? It shows me that all men have the capacity to believe in their minds things they haven't seen with their own eyes. We can believe something is there even though we have never been there to see it. Is this belief or faith? Faith includes belief but it's much more; faith is knowing, and it is acting on our beliefs with confidence because of our experiences. It is a trust. Belief requires no action as it is done with and in the mind, but faith is a matter of the heart that moves us to act a certain way. This tells me that not only are we to believe in Jesus, but we must have faith in Jesus. Billions of people can believe with their minds in other planets, solar systems, the universe, and galaxies; but not until their hearts have been changed through faith can they know and have faith in something or someone greater than those things. His name is Jesus, the savior of the world, and faith in Him is the substance of our hope. In faith, we can see the things we have not seen with our eyes. In faith, we can live the life we have never lived. In faith, we can go to places in God we have never been. In faith, not just believing with our minds

but in our hearts, we can know like we have never known that we are loved.

6. If what we know to be true has never been challenged, then we only have the capacity to regurgitate only what we have been taught and not what we actually know to be true.

7. Some people would rather believe a comfortable lie than to face the uncomfortable truth.

8. The chapter of a life ends on earth, but it begins in eternity. I'm reminded of the fact that bright stars do burn out. According to scientists, the sun, our star in this solar system, shall someday burn out. The lesson we learn when stars fall is that death is everyone's final foe; and that it indiscriminately takes us, mostly, during inconvenient times or times we do not expect. All of our plans, goals, dreams, schedules, and appointments are trumped by this final appointment, an appointment that someday, we all will have and cannot cancel. No amount of money, power, or influence can change this fact. One day, we are here; and the next day, we are gone. *How is it that we know something is going to happen, yet we live as though it will never happen instead of living as though it will happen?* Surprise! Then it happens. There comes a time when we all must come face to face with our own mortality and the reality of exiting this realm and entering another one. While we are here, we should all strive to make a difference and secure life after this life. One day, money and fame will be worthless, but we did with the life were given by the creator will someday be priceless.

9. There is a way that seems good. But underneath it all, cloak in deception, is evil wrapped in what appears to be good but is not God.

10. Living is hard on the body.

11. When I see three crosses, I think about Jesus standing between life and death.

12. *Jesus will come to separate the wheat from the tares (weeds or people who claim and hide behind the church but whose heart*

is not one with the church). "But he said, Nay; lest while ye gather up the tares, ye root up also the wheat with them. Let both grow together until the harvest: and in the time of harvest I will say to the reapers, Gather ye together first the tares, and bind them in bundles to burn them: but gather the wheat into my barn" (Matthew13:29–30)

13. Death doesn't hurt but life does; we are spirits having an earthly experience.

14. At some point in life, we will feel as though we have the world by the tail; but all of a sudden, a season of brokenness appears that causes us to question everything that we thought we knew about ourselves. It is through this view of brokenness we see our depravity and need for the character of God in our lives. It is through this view we see how dependent we are on God for everything. It is through this view we come face to face to who we really are and not the titles or positions we mask our insecurities with. When brokenness fills our cup, everything we have built our image on is poured out. It is through the view of brokenness that God begins to reform and reshape us into what he has called us to. In this view of brokenness, we must look at ourselves until we see the image of God.

15. Under great pressure and heat, a diamond is formed; we must never let the pressures of life or the heat of moments cause us to question our value. Things that press us on every side are the things that are shaping and forming us into something rare and valuable. In the midst of our struggle, we are being changed. If we give up and abort the process, we will never see the beauty that will emerge from the pressure and heat of our pain. We can have hope in knowing that the heat and pressure that causes our pain is never wasted, and it is certainly not the end. It is the necessary beginning of a journey toward being better.

16. Life comes full circle in time; the things we got wrong we will get a chance to make right. If we take, we will get a chance to give. If we take things for granted, we will get

another chance to appreciate those things later. Time has a way of encouraging corrections.

17. We can meet God on the way up, but we only begin to truly know Him on the way down. The further down we go; the stronger the foundation we will have once God begins to rebuild us.

18. If we watch time, more than likely we are wasting it; but if we intentionally slow down to enjoy it, it is time well spent.

19. Never before have we seen the intensity of times such as these. This is a new day, and the sun has set on that which used to be. The weapons against us have been upgraded, so we too must also upgrade our faith and understanding of the times. We must be careful that we be not deceived, for we are living in times of great deception, times full of seducing spirits that will draw many away using the knowledge of their fleshy desires. This anti-Christ spirit gives the deceived platforms to deceive the masses. If we are not careful, we, as sheep, will fall into the line that leads to our own destruction. The only way to guard against deception is to know the Word of God and harken to the voice of the shepherd. We must know the enemy's agenda, but more importantly, be in tune with God's plan. For men have become wise in their own eyes, and in the darkness of their own blindness or understanding, they speak the lies of the deceiver. Be armed with the Word of God, and be led by His Spirit.

20. Tomorrow is yesterday to God, so don't worry. Be happy.

21. Before we allow things to overwhelm us, always remember that in order to build a house, we must start with one board and one nail at a time. We must plan our way forward one step at a time.

22. If truth (the Word of God) is not lost, perhaps something of eternal value will be gained; but when the foundation of truth is erased or ignored, everything that stands will cease to stand and left as remains. The foundation of truth is what holds our chaotic nature together and pushes back

our inherent sorrow. It is the lesson that if not learn today, it shall prove to be our regret tomorrow. If to stand on truth means we must stand alone, then alone is what we must stand on. Truth is as a lamp that will guide us through the shadows of darkness up ahead. It's not relative nor does it change with time, but it is the one constant by which those who are wise are led. That which the blind cannot see behind all of the deception and lies, truth shall always be the standard and the light that gives sight to our eyes. For with it, that which is hidden will be revealed for us to see, the things to come, the things that must and shall be.

23. When we see lots of activity and feel the heat which causes the leaves to reach up to the heavens for rain in their thirst, we know that times are changing. When we see the color of the leaves changing to the best colors of themselves, which are warm, impacting the mood of everything around it, we know that times are changing. When we see the beauty of the leaves in the fall begin to fall, leaving the trees bare, we know that times are changing. When we see the darkness and the coldness that is harsh and most times unforgiving to the bones, we know that, once again, times are changing. When we see the buds on trees awakening and life all around is renewed into what's seems to be a new beginning to that which was, we know that times are changing. Such is that in the spirit realm. There are signs that identify the season we are in. There are signs that remind us of that which was foretold, and there are signs that reveal to us that which is to come. Watch the signs and pray for the new beginning that shall renew the earth and rid us of the influences of darkness.

24. There is nothing we can do to make God love us anymore or any less. Before God, we can be naked and not be ashamed because He sees it all anyway, but yet He stills wants us.

25. Don't drink the Kool-Aid which means that we shouldn't believe everything we hear.

26. This past week, after the storm, many of us experienced life without power; in contrast, how does life differ from not having the power of God operating in our lives? Without the power of God operating in our lives, nothing will ever seem just right. We can't even generate or imitate the power needed to sustain our lives. Without His life on the inside of us, we are already dead. It's just like meat in a powerless freezer; in time, the meat shall rot and be thrown out. Just as we need power operating in our appliances, even more so, we need the power of God operating in our country, our churches, our communities, our schools, our homes, and in our hearts. Without the power of God, which gives light to every dark space of life, we truly would be living in continuous darkness, groping and stumbling over the things we cannot see. We shouldn't wait until the power is out before we understand the value of preparation for the storms of life. For they shall come, but those who are ready (faith, hope, and love) shall have all that they need to get through them.

27. Let not your heart be troubled, but watch and pray. For the days ahead are for the purpose of the victory of the saints. That which has been foretold was told for the preparation of those who believe. Wrath was and never will be meant for the beloved in Christ. We shouldn't close our eyes or faint because of fear, but witness the very reason for the hope of our salvation.

28. Be humble to listen and quick to repent.

29. There is a beginning and ending to everything on earth.

30. In eternity, nothing changes; but in the governing boundaries of time, there are opportunities to change course, to grow, to start over, and in some things to redeem that which has been lost.

31. People say they love us and are praying for us, but there are some walks we have to walk alone, alone with God that is. While we are up wrestling with our situation, they (people) are asleep, but God never sleeps.

32. Disappointments don't define us. In the pursuit of our goals, we shouldn't spend a lot of time looking back because looking back gives failure time to catch up to us. We should invest most our time in what's in our power to change—the path up ahead. Just remember, no one gets ahead running backward!

33. Sometimes, it's not so much of what people say. It is what they don't say that tells us how they really feel.

34. Tears have two different expressions—that of joy and that of sorrow. Unbeknownst to us, they both are one. For if we never know sorrow, we shall never know joy.

35. To everything there is a beginning, a first, and creation date. A rooster and a hen come together to produce an egg that leads to offspring. Who was the first rooster and hen and from whom did they come from? They were created but by whom?

36. We exist for God, and if in our minds we exist for anything else, then we have failed in our existence.

37. The way we can change a generation is by what we teach or not teach children in schools. If we want a faithless and godless generation, we shouldn't mention God. If we want a generation who do not pray, we should remove prayer from schools. The opposite is true if we want God to be the head of our nation and our homes.

38. We can either pray, "Lord, change my situation," or we can pray, "Lord, change me for my situation."

39. Sometimes doing nothing is doing all that needs to be done. It is hard for people of action, but let wisdom guide those actions

40. The problem most of us have is that we feed our bellies more than we feed our minds.

41. The way to avoid a wasted life is to walk in obedience to the Lord.

42. What we don't know gives our enemies everything they need to enslave us.

43. The greatest of all faults is to not be conscious of our own faults.

44. In the end, it will not matter who we know, if we don't know Jesus (Yeshua).

CHAPTER 8

The Fullness of Time:
A New Beginning

OUR DAYS ARE AS THE grass of the field and the flowers of a garden; when winter comes, they all wither away. There is nothing that seems so final than death, but in fact, death is not the final chapter of our existence. It is the end of that which will not last, a lifetime, but the beginning of an existence that which has no end. From start to finish, time always tells a story; and as time passes, we began to understand the full meaning of the story.

Life on earth is like leaving home to go on a long trip, a trip in which we will be staying for an extended undetermined (to us) amount of time. It takes time for us to get acclimated to the new place, but we make the necessary adjustments to get settled in. We have encountered several things in this new place that reminds us of home, but we have come to find that there is no place quite like home. We try to forget about home and focus on our new life; but there is something inside of us, a piece of home, that desires the place from which we came from. As the days go by, this desire grows stronger and stronger to the point that nothing in this new place will satisfy. Home is where the heart is, and until we return home, we will always feel as though something or someone is missing. This thing inside of us that is longing for our return is eternity in our hearts. Our home which is in the Father will always be a part of us. We have a built-in GPS system called time that is taking us back to our beginnings as spirit-beings. To the ground, our earth suits shall return, and who we really are (a spirit being) shall return to the Father's house. To answer the question of where time is taking us, it is taking us to this one auspicious moment when all whoever was and who is stand before the Lamb of God. "Wherefore God also hath highly exalted him, and given him a name which is above every name: That at the name of Jesus every knee should bow, of things in heaven, and things in earth, and things under the earth; and that every tongue should confess that Jesus Christ is Lord, to the glory of God the Father" (Philippians 2:9–11). *In a full circle, time is taking us home sweet home to the Father's house for the consummation of the groom and the bride into holy matrimony. Time is the preparation period of the bride. We are preparing to go to a wedding.*

The Earth Shall Remain

Throughout this journey, we have been guided by an internal time piece that manages our existence here on the earth by getting us from one moment to the next. By placing our hand over our chest, we can feel time moving us along one beat at a time. We all are one heartbeat away from death and eternity. As in almost all things in this realm, time and our journey on earth will eventually end, but this world (earth) shall never end.

> One generation passeth away, and another generation cometh: but the earth abideth for ever. (Ecclesiastes 1:4)

From the genesis of our creation up to this moment in time, God has remained committed to fulfilling His purpose for the earth. The biblical story of creation did not start with the ugliness of sin, but it started with the genius and creativity of God shaping the earth into one of His most beautiful masterpieces. Even to this day, in the fallen state of sin, the earth, in its beauty, I'm sure, is still the envy of our universe. The earth was made perfect for man, and given to him to have dominion or sovereign authority over it according to Genesis. As the story goes, man, through his disobedience to God, gave his sovereign authority over to a serpent that was possessed by a devil. As a result, man went from being ruler to being ruled; and as a result of their sin against God, He was required, because of justice, to pay the only price that could be paid for sin—death. The definition of death is simply separation from the body; but this death, as a result of sin, is separation from God. We can either spend eternity with God or eternity separated from God. Separation from God is separation from life because God is life; this is what it means to be spiritually dead. Justice demands a life for a life. If we take the life God has given us and separate ourselves from Him, justice demands that in order for our lives to be redeemed, a worthy sacrifice must be given, and the only worthy sacrifice to God is the innocent blood of His Son who knew no sin. Man was spiritually dead and, in his fallen state, doomed for a natural earthly death. As God had planned from the very beginning, He would wrap Himself in flesh, as the Word (Jesus His son), and redeem humanity by the shedding of His innocent blood. The body would die (just as man's body will die) and be the price paid in full once and for all. The Son took back the keys (authority) of death, hell, and the grave and rose on the third day with all power. He redeemed that which was lost, the earth, and then He returned to the Father only to someday soon return to redeem that which He paid for (His bride). "The earth is the Lord's, and the fulness thereof; the world, and they that dwell therein" (Psalm 24).

> And when I saw him, I fell at his feet as dead. And he laid his right hand upon me, saying unto me, Fear not; I am the first and the last: I am he that liveth, and was dead; and, behold, I am alive for evermore, Amen; and have the keys of hell and of death. (Revelation 1:17–18)

While on the earth before He died, rose on the third day, and ascended to His Father in heaven, Jesus told his disciples, in John 13:36, that where He was going, they could not follow Him right away. At that time, Jesus was on his way to the cross to pay the price for all (past, present, and future) of humanity's sins. This was something that He had to do alone because no one else could bear the cup he was about to drink. No one else could bear the sins of the world. One could only imagine the devastation His disciples must have felt because they gave up everything to follow him, and now, His talk of leaving them must have felt as though they were being abandoned. I believe Jesus could sense the secret conversations in their hearts, so this is what he said to them.

> Let not your heart be troubled: ye believe in God, believe also in me. In my Father's house are many mansions: if it were not so, I would have told you. I go to prepare a place for you. And if I go and prepare a place for you, I will come again, and receive you unto myself; that where I am, there ye may be also. (John 14:1–3)

This response by Jesus was expressed to them in a way that his disciples culturally understood. It is believed that Jesus used their understanding of the Jewish wedding rituals to explain His intentions and purpose in the earth. According to John 14:29, Jesus told them this, before it came to pass, that when it did come to pass, they would remember and believe what he had told them.

The Parallel of the Jewish Wedding

There is a parallel between a Jewish wedding and the return of Christ. Those who believe in Christ and the price He paid for them are considered the bride of Christ. According to Revelation 19, our time on earth is a time of preparation as a bride (the church or believers) with the promise of Christ (the groom) to return to take us to the marriage ceremony and the marriage supper of the Lamb that will be celebrated at the Father's house (heaven). The ancient Jewish wedding rituals are symbolic to the wedding believers who have been invited when all of heaven witness Jesus taking His bride. According to Jewish wedding customs at the time of Jesus's earthly ministry, there was a process that included five stages that led to the completion of the marriage:

The marriage arrangements—an agreement between two families to match a groom and a bride. A contract is written up depicting the terms and conditions of the marriage arrangement, the responsibilities, and obligations of both parties and the dowry to be offered.

The betrothal (the promise)—both the bride and the groom were immersed in water, vow to be married, exchange something of value, and sealed the agreement by sharing a cup of wine. At this point, they were legally married even though they were not to live in the same house or have sexual relations yet. They were to return to their father's house until the time of preparation was complete.

The preparation period between the betrothal and the wedding—the groom remained at his father's home and prepared a place for the two to live. This was normally done by adding a room to his father's house. While the groom was building, the bride was preparing herself for the upcoming wedding. She was observed for purity which required at least a full nine months to pass to ensure that the bride was not pregnant. Then, she consecrated herself by changing anything that needed changing in her life (activities and relationships included) for her marriage. Last but not least, she had to make her own garment. They didn't have dress shops back then. They spent hours adorning her garment with special touches to make it beautiful, hence the phrase, "without spot or blemish," in a spiritual sense as referred to the bride of Christ.

The wedding ceremony—toward the end of the year-long betrothal period, the bride waited with great expectancy for the return of the groom and for the ceremony to take place. Even late in the evening, the bridal party and the bride had to keep oil in their lamps just in case the groom returned. The day of the ceremony was a surprise to the groom and to the bride because no one knew the day or the hour except the father. Once it was time, the friends of the groom would shout "Behold the bridegroom comes," and then they would blow the shofar. After the ceremony, the couple consummated or sealed the marriage with sexual relations. They became one flesh.

The wedding feast—this was the highlight of the wedding ceremony. It consisted of *seven full days* (while there is seven years of tribulation on the earth) of food, music, dance, and celebration. The primary purpose of the wedding feast at the father's house is to honor the groom. The bride would honor the groom by displaying her beautiful wedding garments that she spent a year preparing to all of those in attendance. After the wedding feast, the groom and the bride lived together as husband and wife for the remainder of their lives.

> Let us be glad and rejoice, and give honour to him: for the marriage of the Lamb is come, and his wife hath made herself ready. And to her was granted that she should be arrayed in fine linen, clean and white: for the fine linen is the righteousness of saints. And he saith unto me, Write, Blessed are they which are called unto the marriage supper of the Lamb. And he saith unto me, These are the true sayings of God. (Revelation 19:7–9)

In comparison to the ancient Jewish wedding system, believers in Christ are halfway through the process of being married to the Lamb of God whom redeemed us by paying the bridal price with His life. That is the value God placed on us. Those of us who have accepted the bridal price are in the stage of preparation, much like an ancient Jewish bride. As with the ancient Jewish wedding customs, Jesus, the bridegroom, will come at a day and hour that his bride nor himself knows; only the Father knows. The bride, which is the church or believers, must be ready at all times.

> For the Lord himself shall descend from heaven with a shout, with the voice of the archangel, and with the trump of God: and the dead in Christ shall rise first: Then we which are alive and remain shall be caught up together with them in the clouds, to meet the Lord in the air: and so shall we ever be with the Lord. (1 Thessalonians 4:16–17)

Jesus's first coming was like the arrangement of marriage in the Jewish wedding system. Every born-again believer is betrothed to Jesus as his bride, and while we wait for the bridegroom to return, we live in the period of preparation. This time of preparation will end at the appointed time of the Father, once the Father tells the son to go get His bride, once the voice of the archangel and the trump of God is sounded; the bride will be caught up in the air to be with the bridegroom, and the restrainer (the Holy Spirit) will be taken away. The wedding ceremony and the marriage feast of the Lamb will then take place. It will last the length of the period of tribulation (*seven full years*) on the earth. After the end of seven years, Jesus will return to the earth to judge the nations, establish His kingdom, and rule the earth. As in the Jewish wedding tradition, the earth shall be an extension of the Father's house. The New Jerusalem shall descend, and Christ and his bride shall rule and reign. The earth is the Lord's.

A New Heaven and New Earth

> And before him shall be gathered all nations: and he shall separate them one from another, as a shepherd divideth his sheep from the goats: And he shall set the sheep on his right hand, but the goats on the left. Then shall the King say unto them on his right hand, Come, ye blessed of my Father, inherit the kingdom prepared for you from the foundation of the world. (Matthew 25:32–34)

As we live and breathe, governments and human efforts to achieve peace on earth has and will always fail. The earth will never have peace until the Prince of Peace (Jesus) puts an end to the rebellion of Satan and his fallen angels' reign on earth. According to Genesis 1 of the Holy Bible, time, the first day, was established by the separation of darkness and light. When the fullness of time comes, God will finally, once and for all, separate darkness from light and evil from good. Time is simply the transition between this change and the vehicle for God's purpose to be fulfilled.

In the beginning, the creator had a glorious plan for the earth. The entrance of sin did not change God's plan. The earth shall remain, but according to 2 Peter 3: 10, it will be purified by fire to restore it to its original glory. When Jesus returns to the earth at the end of the marriage supper of the Lamb, He will not be alone; he will return with the armies of heaven (Revelation 19:14) to the earth to rule and reign in what is called the Millennium or thousand-year reign. During this time, Satan will be bound for one thousand years (Revelation 20:1–3), and the saints will reign for one thousand years (Revelation 20:4–6). Satan will then be released, and he will lead, as he always does, his final rebellion (Revelation 20:7–9). After Christ puts an end to this rebellion and Satan and all of his followers stand before God at the Great White Throne Judgment (Revelation 20:11–15), Satan and His followers will be tormented forever in the lake of fire (Revelation 20:10).

The world to come is mentioned in the books of Isaiah 65:17 and 66:22, 2 Peter 3:13, and Revelation 21 of the Holy Bible. The world to come will be as it was from the beginning—perfect. At time's end and eternity's beginning, we will also see a new heaven and a new earth as depicted and described in Revelation 21:1–8.

> And I saw a new heaven and a new earth: for the first heaven and the first earth were passed away; and there was no more sea. And I John saw the holy city, new Jerusalem, coming down from God out of heaven, prepared as a bride adorned for her husband. And I heard a great voice out of heaven saying, Behold, the tabernacle of God is with men, and he will dwell with them, and they shall be his people, and God himself shall be with them, and be their God. And God shall wipe away all tears from their eyes; and there shall be no more death, neither sorrow, nor crying, neither shall there be any more pain: for the

former things are passed away. And he that sat upon the throne said, Behold, I make all things new. And he said unto me, Write: for these words are true and faithful. And he said unto me, It is done. I am Alpha and Omega, the beginning and the end. I will give unto him that is athirst of the fountain of the water of life freely. He that overcometh shall inherit all things; and I will be his God, and he shall be my son. But the fearful, and unbelieving, and the abominable, and murderers, and whoremongers, and sorcerers, and idolaters, and all liars, shall have their part in the lake which burneth with fire and brimstone: which is the second death. (Revelation 21:1–8)

This is the conclusion of the greatest story ever told. This troubled planet will finally experience peace, and this is just the beginning of the joy of belonging to Christ. We who are in Christ are not finished when time runs out. But we will just start over, and things will be the way God intended them to be from the beginning. Sadly, the journey of those not found in Christ will end when time expires and when there is no need for the sun and the moon; there will be no "new beginning or new earth" experience for those who reject Christ; they will be forever separated from life—separate from God into complete darkness. God will finally put an end to rebellion. Satan, those who follow him, and the influence of darkness shall be no more.

And there shall be no night there; and they need no candle, neither light of the sun; for the Lord God giveth them light: and they shall reign for ever and ever. (Revelation 22:5)

The proclivity of time or the natural course of time goes one way, and that is from the beginning to the end. But there is a supernatural course of time beyond what we see and fully know. *As spirit being, we never really come to an end; we just transition from a temporal state of time to an eternal state of being.*

> Having made known unto us the mystery of his will, according to his good pleasure which he hath purposed in himself: That in the dispensation of the fulness of times he might gather together in one all things in Christ, both which are in heaven, and which are on earth; even in him: In whom also we have obtained an inheritance, being predestinated according to the purpose of him who worketh all things after the counsel of his own will. (Ephesians 1:9–11)

God's kingdom is coming to the earth. The will of God shall be done on earth as it is in heaven, and that, my friend, is the proclivity of time. Full circle, time is taking us back to the beginning.

Selah 8:1–44

1. Time is not just that was or that will be; it is until it is no more.
2. There is no my truth or your truth; there is only the truth which is the Word of God (the Bible). Also, just because something is true (laced with a lie) does not necessarily mean it's truth. His Word is the only standard from which we should measure anything, and just because we tell people the truth doesn't mean we are trying to be the judge. To judge, we have to sit above and see the situation from a high place. Now if we put "ourselves" in this high place, we are sure to fall ourselves. The truth (God's Word) judges (measures right or wrong) all on its own. The problem comes in when we lose sight that we should take that same truth and measure our own hearts as often as possible. While measuring, we would be reminded of the fact that more often than we care to admit, we all have fallen short of the mark.

This doesn't exempt us from speaking truth (warnings) in love because when truth which is light is no longer seen or heard, darkness with its lies and deception traps and tries to keep the blind away from the truth. Truth makes us conscious of what needs to be made right in us, but it is love that leads us to freedom. Speak the truth in love.

3. As the old song goes "One of these ole days, I'm going to put on my role and tell my story of how I made it over." Each moment, each day, and each year, we write the stories of our lives; and someday, it shall be read back to us. It's up to us to make sure this story victorious; it's up to us to make sure our lives are well lived. It's up to us to make sure that someday we hear these words: "Enter my rest thy good and faithful servant." Always, remember that we live in the world we create; better choices equal a better life.

4. Life is made up of opposite experiences which balance each other.

5. What we have done is not as important as what He (Jesus) has done. He paid the debts of our past so that we could have a guaranteed future. All we have to do is let go of our pride and receive the receipt of that payment. It's the only way we can receive a full refund on life.

6. Government is man's feeble attempt to save us, but only Jesus can truly save us. It would be wise to never lose sight that our faith and hope for the future should be in Him alone, and no matter who wins, we can never lose because of our faith. The ballots have already been casted and counted, yet the race has already been won at the cross! We, "the people of the Book," win! Now, let's celebrate by giving Jesus thanks today for our victory in Him tomorrow! Amen.

7. God has always been God, and God is still God. There is no need to be fearful of the future because come what may, God will still be God!

8. Does not the lives of the unborn matter? Regardless of race, their blood cries up from the ground to our creator; will

He not hear them? Will He not avenge them and balance the scale? Will He not secure justice for those who have no voice? Is not justice for all? Where is the outcry? Who will take up this cause? This issue is very personal to God, and those who promote and support those who promote this agenda put themselves in opposition with God. There is a curse associated with taking "innocent" life. Do we dare sacrifice our babies to the God of ourselves and our convenience? We dare justify murder by declaring it's our right to do so. Thank God our mothers believed we had a right to live; otherwise, our blood would be crying up to the heavens and the scent of blood would be forever fresh upon their hands. This is a stain on our conscience and our nation that cannot be erased until we repent. It won't be erased until we put an end to this offense to God. Where is the fear of the Holy God? God is not mocked! Whatsoever we sow, we shall reap. Do not be surprised by the trouble in our land. If only as nation we would turn back to God, how much more blessed we would be!

9. We pay a lot a money to portray an image that won't keep.

10. In one word, what is the whole point of our existence? I surmise that it is love. It was the reason why we were created. It is why we are here to accept it; and one day, because of the sacrifice that love requires, we shall know love like we have never known it before.

11. Sometimes, we have to touch the bottom or come to the end of ourselves in order to see where we have come from, where we are, and where we are going.

12. We can expect bad weather, but we can also expect the sun to shine again. Time brings everything to its end, and the way to avoid a wasted life is to walk in obedience to the Lord.

13. A course unchanged assures the end. The course of life teaches us to the end. When the lesson is over, whether we got it or not, we still must go home.

14. How dark does it have to get for us to see the light? There is a call that is going out: Come out of the deception of

religion. Come out of the traditions of man. Come out of atheism and humanism. Come out of the bars for the emptiness that we try to fill shall never be full. "Come out of the lifestyles of perversion for we were created in my image says the Lord. Come out of idolatry for I shall have no other God before me." Our money burns, and then it is no more. Our material things, in time, loses their appeal. The images we have placed on a pedestal shall fall, and the things we hold dear outside of Jesus shall not last.

15. A heartbeat is the only thing that stands between us and eternity. This truth is regardless of what we believe. Time will be over for us once the heart stops. Then we will either be in the presence of God, or we will lift up our eyes in hell. Tomorrow will never come, and our hour of salvation will have passed. While there is still time, our hour of salvation is now. We must repent, turn away from that which offends God, and ask for forgiveness. We must believe and confess with our mouth that Jesus died for our sins. We must receive His gift of life to us, and finally we must give thanks and share that gift with others!

16. Time is tricky in the fact that it passes whether or not we are conscious of it.

17. Love everyone; love them enough to tell them about Jesus.

18. Faith is not inherited from our parents or grandparents; it's grown. It is a seed that God has already planted in us a measure of. It is our responsibility to pray, to hear the Word of God, to exercise (practice) our faith, to surrender our will, to place our hope in God, to use situations in life to grow our faith in God. We have stewardship of the power given to us to move mountains and to move the heart of God. After all, it is impossible to please Him without it. Our level of growth determines our level of faith and God's level of pleasure in us.

19. The one who does not know what he is missing never misses it, so the next time someone says, "You don't know what you are missing," say, "You are right, so don't tell me."

20. For those of us who are married and we feel as though our marriage is boring and we are missing out on something, we are not missing anything; it's all an illusion. Well, I take that back; we are missing out on diseases, children out of wedlock, heartbreak, headache, and temporary "love." Be careful not to miss out on salvation. The devil hates marriage, and he will deceive us into thinking that the grass is greener. At some point, all grass turns brown. Here is a little word of wisdom. We should water our own grass, stay in our own yard, and play on our own field.

21. We should ask God to fill us with His joy. It's not like happiness because it's not based on circumstances. The joy of the Lord is our strength. When our power goes out, his joy is like a generator sustaining us until we come back online. It's okay to feel vulnerable and weak, but we must remember to run to the Father and let Him renew us. His grace (the ability to do what we can't do in our own strength) is sufficient (more than enough to sustain us). He will get us through this if we just stay in His presence and listen only to His voice. Our victory will be His victory and when we share it, it will be the victory of others. Everything we have need of is in Him, and it's ours if we want it because he loves us. We don't have to fight; we only need to hold Abba's hand, and He will fight for us! He turns our ashes into something beautiful! Sometimes, we must shout for joy and sing ourselves free from oppression. We must believe that better days are ahead!

22. Sometimes, things don't happen for us when we want them to happen, and the change we long for remains the same. What do we do when that which we hoped for don't come? Trust God anyway! Trust that God Has a plan for our lives. Trust that He knows which direction our lives and circumstances surrounding our lives must go to get us where He is taking us. We must ride the wave until we find ourselves safely ashore. When we feel as though there is no ground under our feet and we are falling, we must stand upon our

faith in a God that will never let our foot slip, but He will carry us and take each step with us. Contrary to how we feel and what we tell ourselves, we are never alone. Look to the Father because His eyes never turn from us!

23. Everyone is entitled to their own opinion, but no one is entitled to their own truth. There is only one truth, and that is in Jesus Christ.

24. There is a falling away of marriage, of manhood, and of womanhood. Women want to be men; men want to be women, and many refuse to marry. It is a state of confusion.

25. What will cause the world to hate God's people? The world in its darkness hates the light—it hates the truth.

26. Don't let the waves of life just crash upon you, but in time, learn to ride the waves ashore.

27. We measure our lives by time, but God measures it by purpose.

28. We can run in place and never get anywhere, what makes the difference in our running is found in our decision to go somewhere.

29. There is a kingdom of darkness out there, and if we flirt with the devil, it won't be long until we will have one to deal with. The language of the enemy is fear. Don't speak his language nor celebrate anything that give glory to him. Sometimes, we wonder why we can't get victory. Well, it's because we have invited the enemy into our house; and his agenda is to steal, kill, and destroy. We even, in the name of fun, introduce him to our children. We must stand at our gates and not let the Trojan horse in. Though it may seem harmless, it will destroy our lives and homes. #histricknotreat

30. May the blessing of God remain with America for our support of Israel! Whatever we do to the Jewish people shall be done unto us!

31. The value of anything is determined by how rare it can be found. Being that there is no one on earth like us makes us

very valuable. We must know our worth to the kingdom of God and live accordingly.

32. Wasted time is wasted life

33. The value of what we do is found in the experiences we gained. Time is not wasted if there is something gained in the experience.

34. Emmanuel—God is with us no matter the situation; He is never absent from the scene. He is behind the scene, working and turning the situation around for our good. We may wonder, *What good can come from this?* The people wondered if any good thing could come from Nazareth. God has the distinct ability to turn a hopeless situation into hope. He can create things with nothing to start with. He can make a way out of no way. There is no situation beyond God's ability to speak life into it. No matter how far we try to run from Him, He is there waiting for our return. He saves us from situations we don't even know we need saving from. When people have given up on us, Emmanuel still believes in us; and believe it or not, He still wants us. Nothing can separate us from His love because He is love, and He is always there. It is impossible for us not to be loved. His mercy endures forever! That's enough to shout about!

35. When we magnify something, the spirit of that thing shows up.

36. Two sides: one, Jesus writes on the sand! "He who is without sin cast the first stone He says." We all need to walk away to examine our own actions and our own lives. Maybe then, we all will put down the stones we have been carrying to judge those who have sinned against us. The fingers we have pointed can't heal, but His finger rewrites the story; it's called forgiveness! No side can accuse the other because we are all guilty of something. "Go and sin no more."

37. There is a beginning and ending to everything except God.

38. That which divides us has the potential to destroy us. It's up to us!

39. Time has an answer for all of our questions. It will always report from the beginning to the end. In time, mysteries are revealed, and that which is unfinished shall be fulfilled. Time holds most of what there is to know; the rest we shall know once we reach the borders beyond the end.

40. When Jesus walked the earth, people were so offended about the people he associated with that they were blinded to the fact that they were in the midst of God's plan and will. Their own will were more important to the point that they missed Him. Be not offended who God is using and what He is doing. He will not always show up the way we expect him to. He uses people and situations for His purpose and not ours.

41. Our past can't survive our future unless we breathe life into it.

42. We can't change the truth, but the truth can change us.

43. We should not be moved by the darkness we see, for in the end, God will get the glory!

44. If living for God with the time I have is not my priority, then my life is wasted, and I have failed in my existence.

The Final Hour

Time synchronizes the events in our lives, and everything comes together in the end according to God's plan. Let us not forget the return of the Lord is imminent (at any moment now) and more so in the days now that we live in. We are in the final hour, and all the preparations have been made. The stage has been set, and all of the guests have been invited. Those who have accepted the invitation, only now, await the start of the ceremony. The day we have long waited for is here, and in this final hour, time will stop and forever shall never end. Beyond the veil of limitation, which is time, there is no past, present, or future; only forever.

Time is a gift from a loving Father who is merciful and patient in His judgment!

BIBLIOGRAPHY

Caldera, Camille. "Homicide Trends in the U.S., 1980–2008." *USA Today*, U.S. Department of Justice, Bureau of Justice Statistics. November 2011.

Edwards, Gene. *The Beginning*. SeedSowers Publishers, 2003.

Goodloe, J. Mills, and Salvador Paskowitz. "The Age of Adaline." 2015.

Hearst Magazine Media. of the Most Powerful Martin Luther King Jr. Quotes by Mckenzie Jean-Philippe." www.hearst.com.

Hebert, David. 2006. The Rapture of the Church: A Doctrine of the Early Church or a Recent Development of the Dispensational Movement.

King James Version of the Holy Bible, Oxford, printed at the University Press London in 1876; Henry Frowne Oxford University Press Warehouse 7, New York. 42 Bleecher Street. https://en.m.wikipedia.org/wiki/New_Earth_(Christianity).

Ladd, George Eldon. *The Last Things, An Eschatology for Laymen*. Grand Rapids: Wm. B. Eerdmans Publishing Co., 1978. (84. Rosenthal, 53. Zodhiates, "harpazo," Dictionary, 257.)

Mark Correll Ministries. "What to Do If You Miss the Rapture." In the News. September 13, 2020

Peterson, Nolan. "China Experimenting on Humans to Engineer Biologically Enhanced Soldiers," Top US Intel Officials says. December 04, 2020

Prophecy News Watch. P.O. Box 3394 Hayden, Idoho 83835

ScienceDaily. University of Helsinki. April 15, 2005.

Smith, Troy L. Cleveland.com. "Stop Using 'Black-on-Black' Crime to Deflect Away from Police Brutality." June 23, 2020.

Tomorrow's World. September–October 2020. TomorrowsWorld. org

"What Is Time?" University of Helsinki: w.sciencedaily.com. Wikipedia. April 15, 2005. https://www.wikipedia.org/

ABOUT THE AUTHOR

DARNELL WHITTINGTON HAS SERVED AS a vice principal for many years in Monroe, Louisiana. He holds a bachelor of science degree and a master's degree in education from the University of Louisiana at Monroe. He has authored several books, served on the board of directors for the Assembly Church of West Monroe and the Voice Network Television station, but his greatest accomplishments are accepting Jesus Christ and building a family which includes Justice and Anita Chatzistrati Whittington.

CPSIA information can be obtained
at www.ICGtesting.com
Printed in the USA
BVHW062023011221
622865BV00006B/180